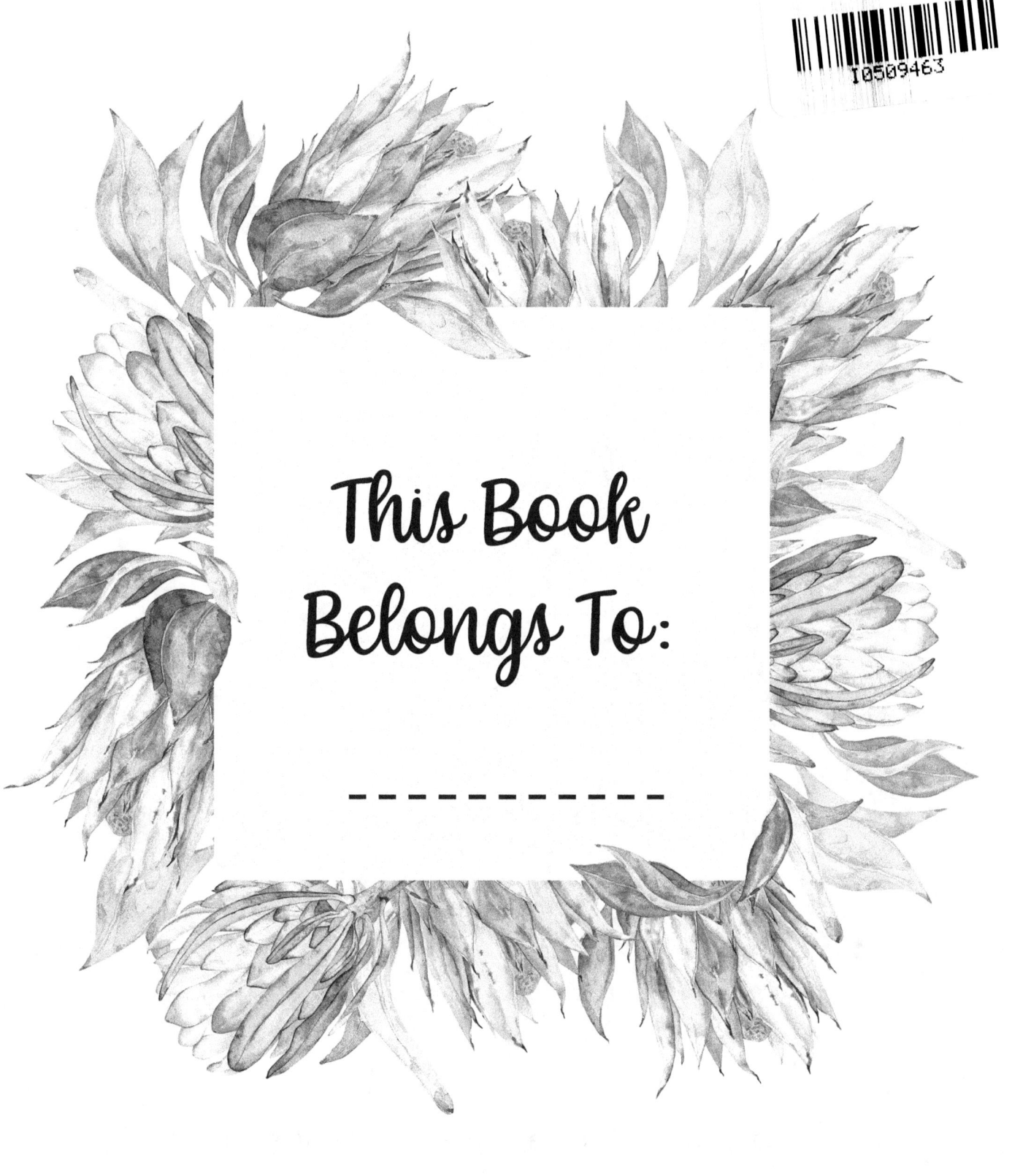

Copyright © Kreative Kolor - All Rights Reserved

No part of this publication may be reproduced, stored in a retrieval system, or transmitted in any form or by any means, electronic, mechanical, photocopying, recording or otherwise, without the prior written permission of the publisher.

How To Color Your Grayscale Pictures

When coloring over grayscale the gray is intended as your guide. Another way is to imagine your picture as an adult color by numbers without the numbers. Instead the darkness or lightness of the gray tells you how dark or light a color to use and where to apply it. Basically you just need to remember, light colors over light grays, dark colors over dark grays and medium colors in between to seamlessly blend light and dark.

Just A Few Tips:

Remember to use your dark colors sparingly when you start. You can make them darker easily darker but it's not so easy to lighten them.

Even if a part of your uncolored picture seems extremely dark you can and should still go over it with a dark color. It will make it pop and really help bring your image to life.

You can go heavy with your lights right away, if you prefer.

One way to start is by doing your lights and then your darks or darks first then lights, whichever you are most comfortable with.

When you apply your medium colors don't be afraid to color on top of your already applied lights and darks the objective is to nicely blend everything. You will find that the lights and darks show through your medium colors. That's not to say you should cover everything with your medium color but instead that it's ok if there is overlap where needed as it will help with the blending and the detail will not be lost.

Your picture doesn't have to be perfect . You will be amazed by how the grayscale is helpful not only in providing a guide but also how it enhances your final picture.

COLOR TESTER

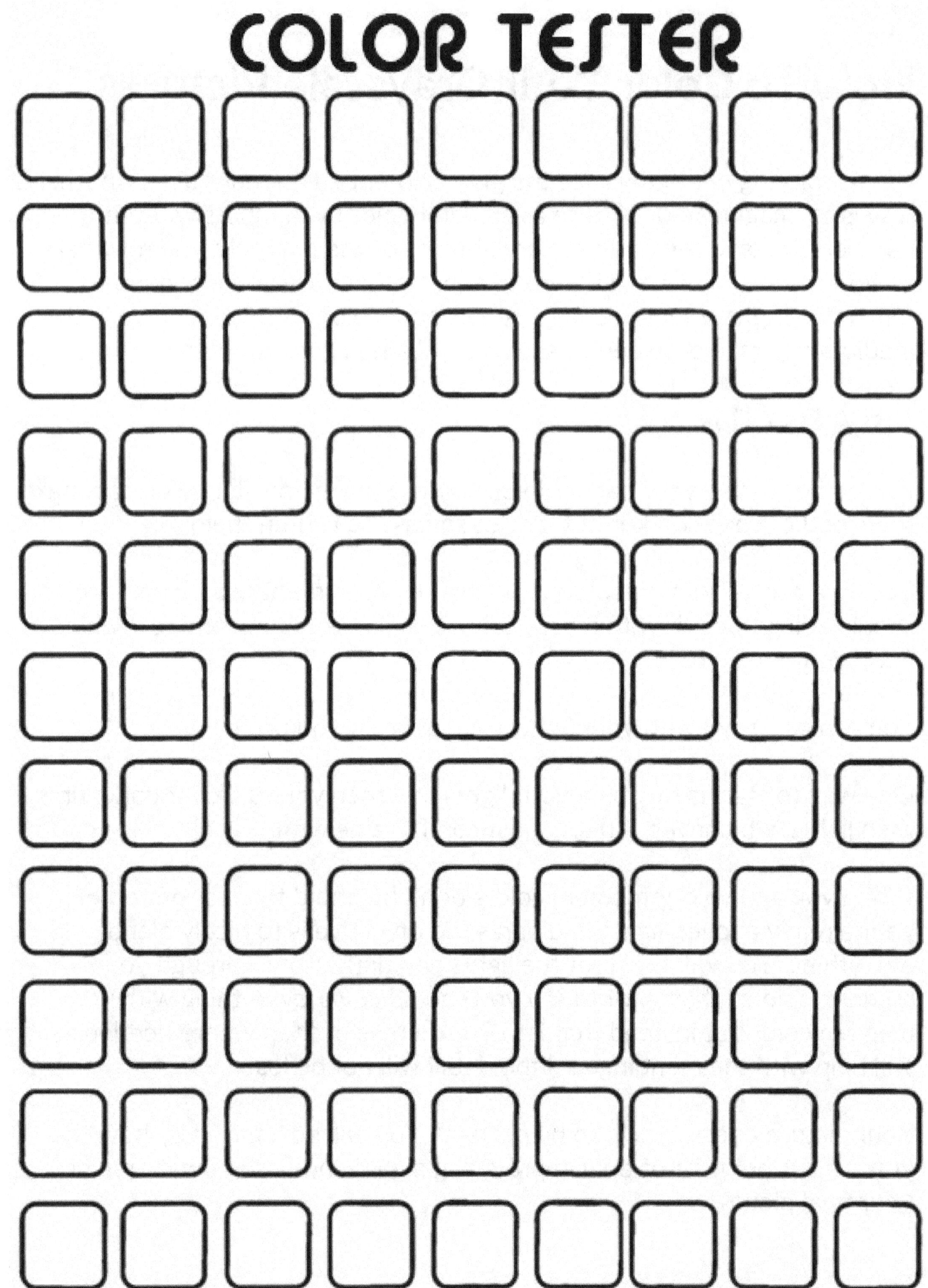

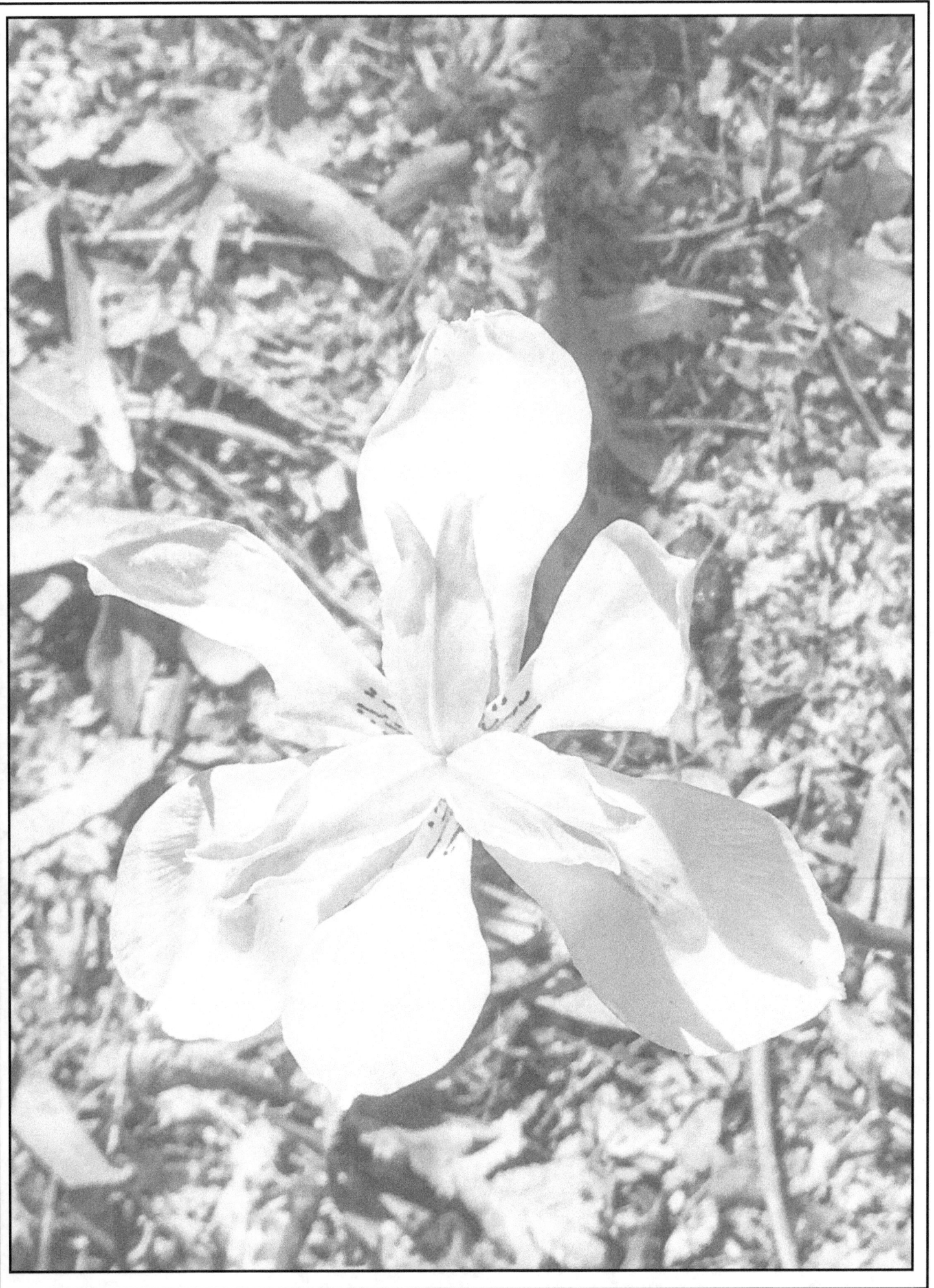

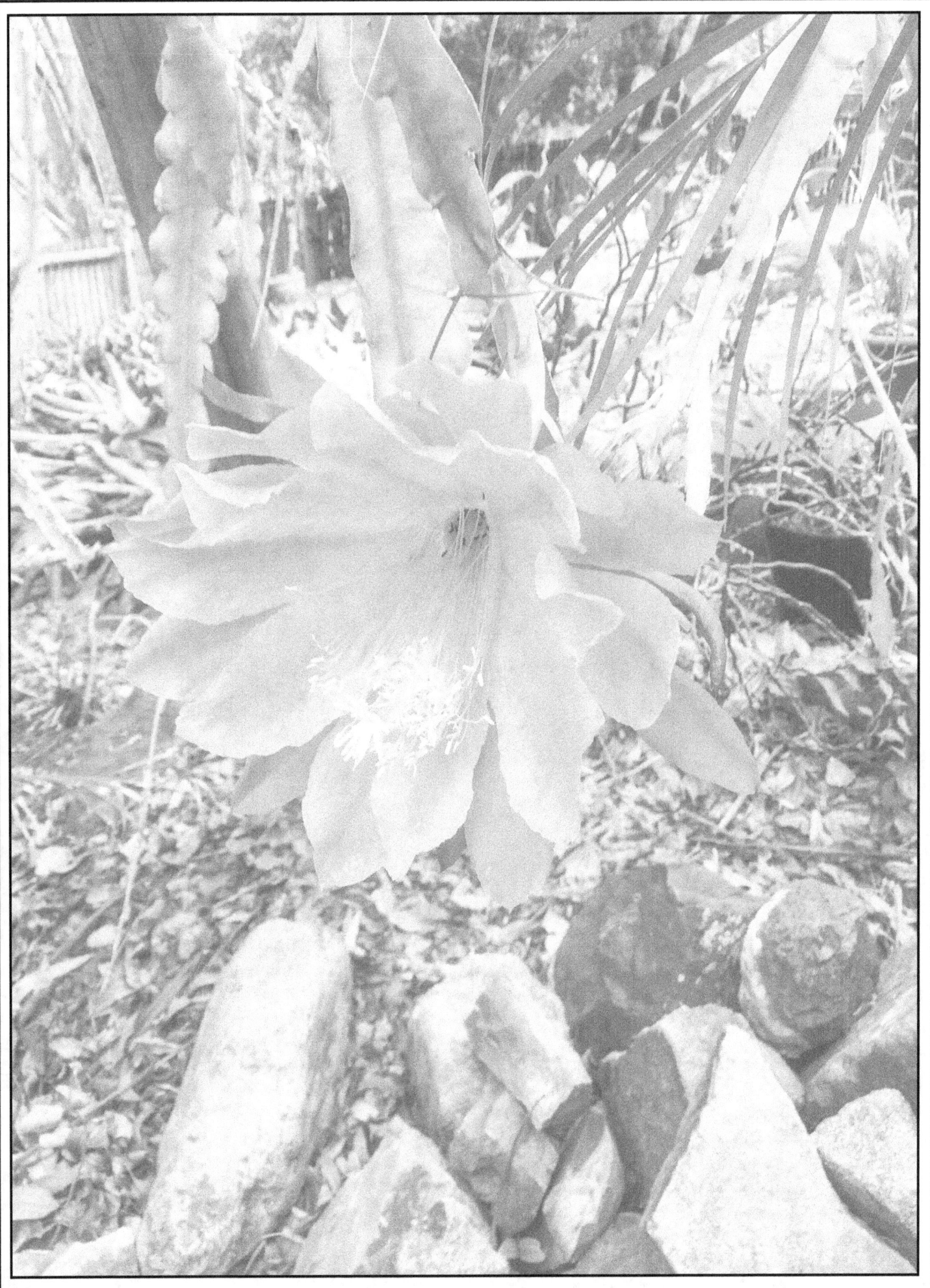

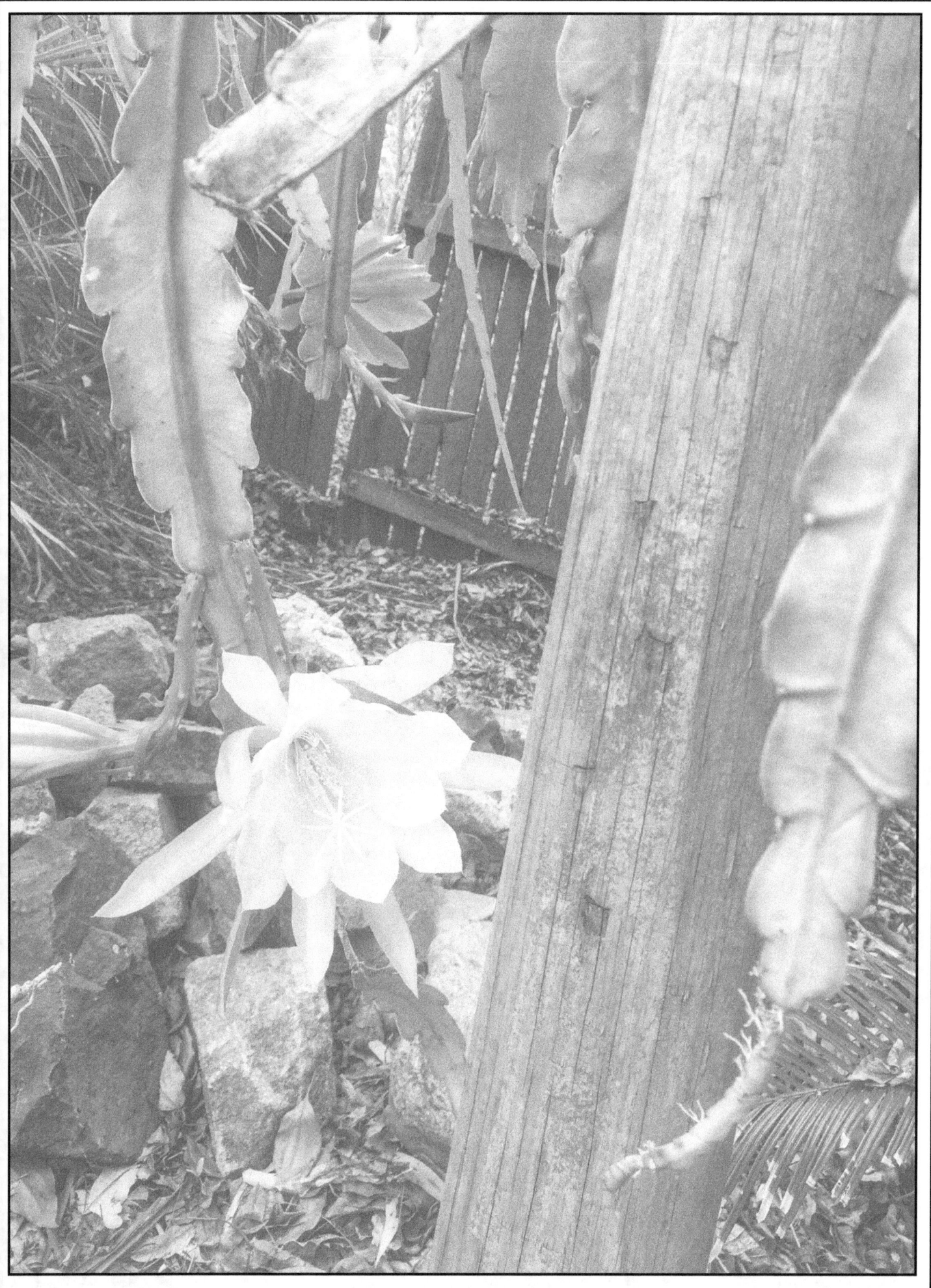

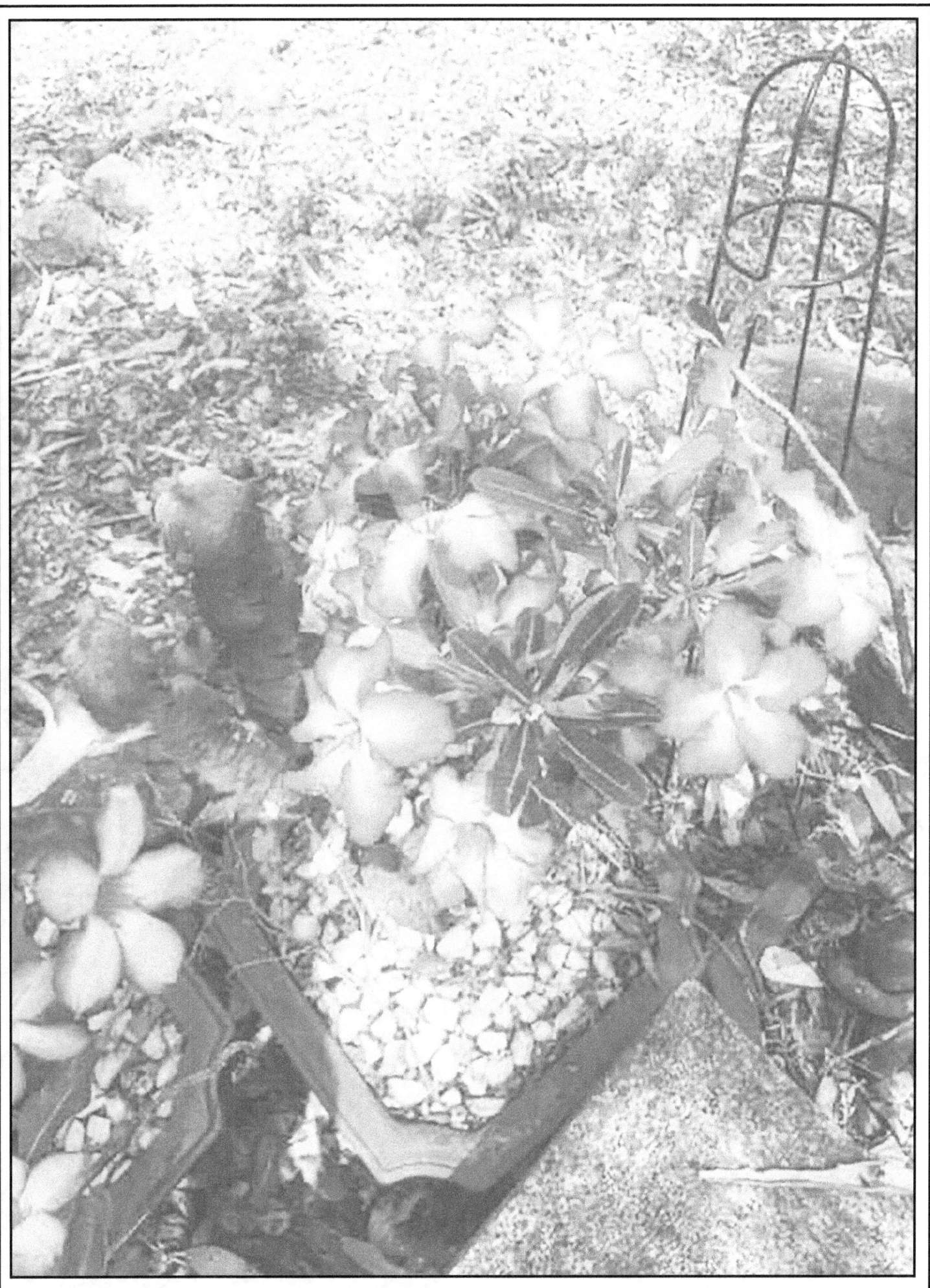

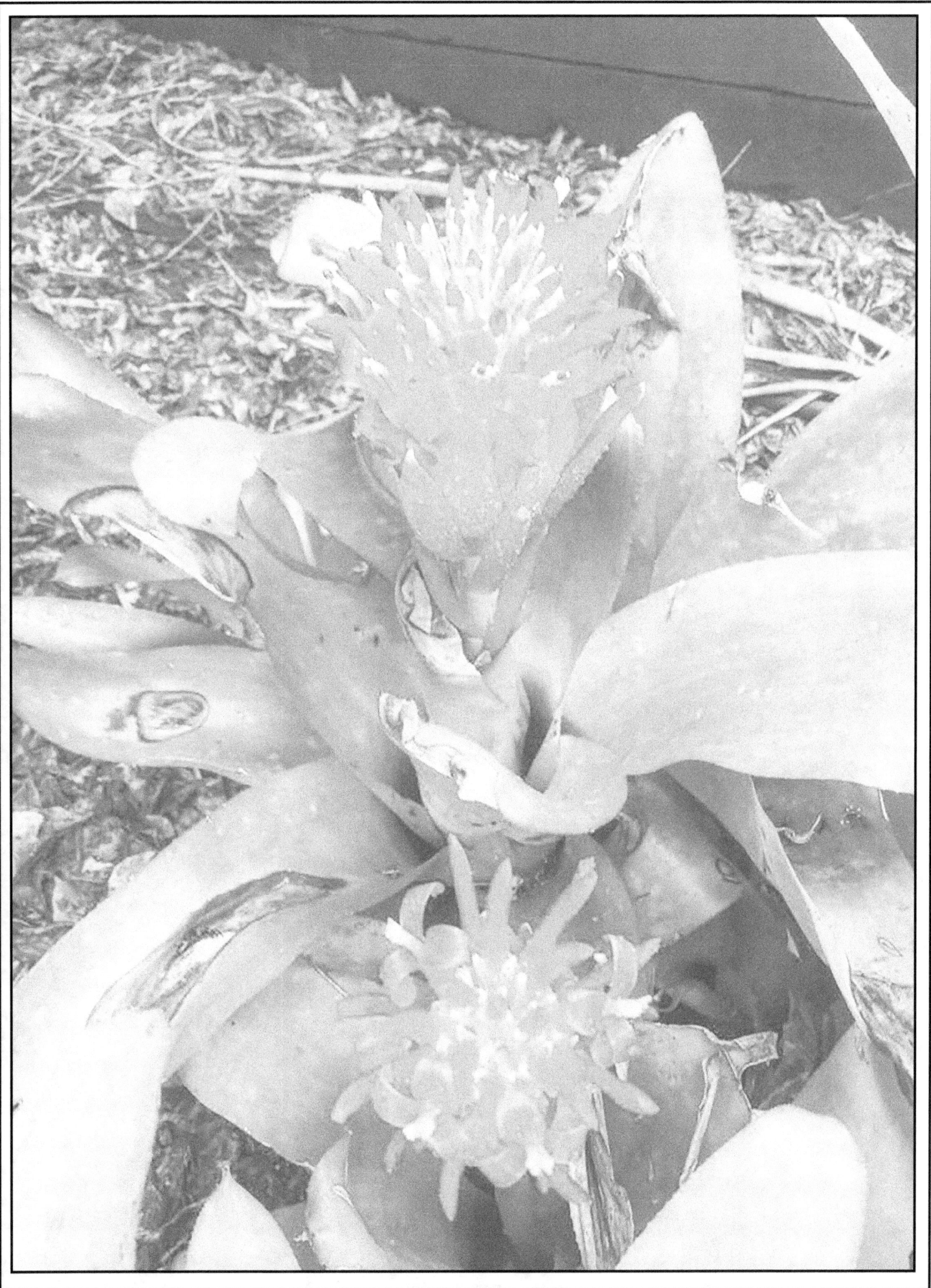

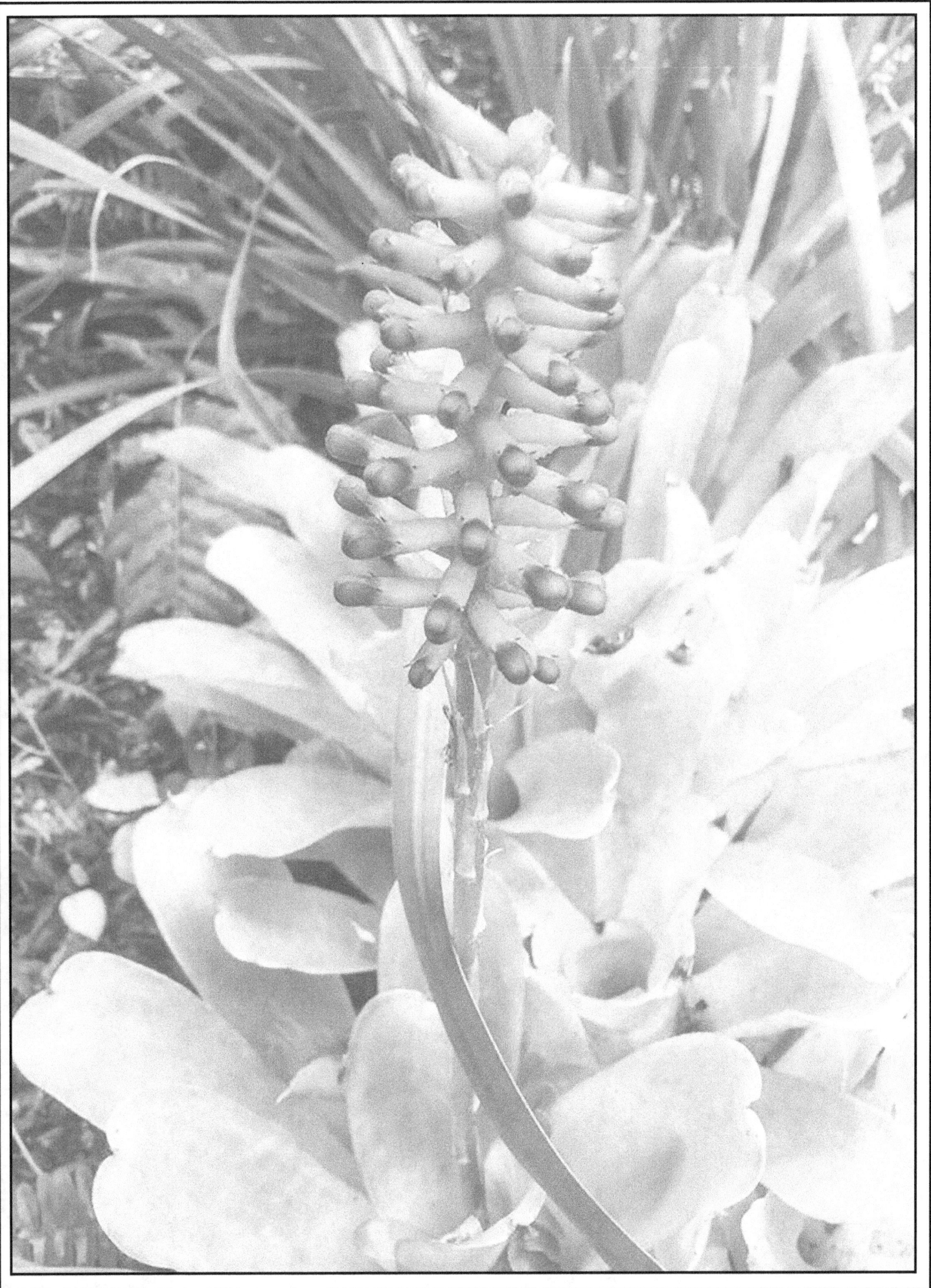

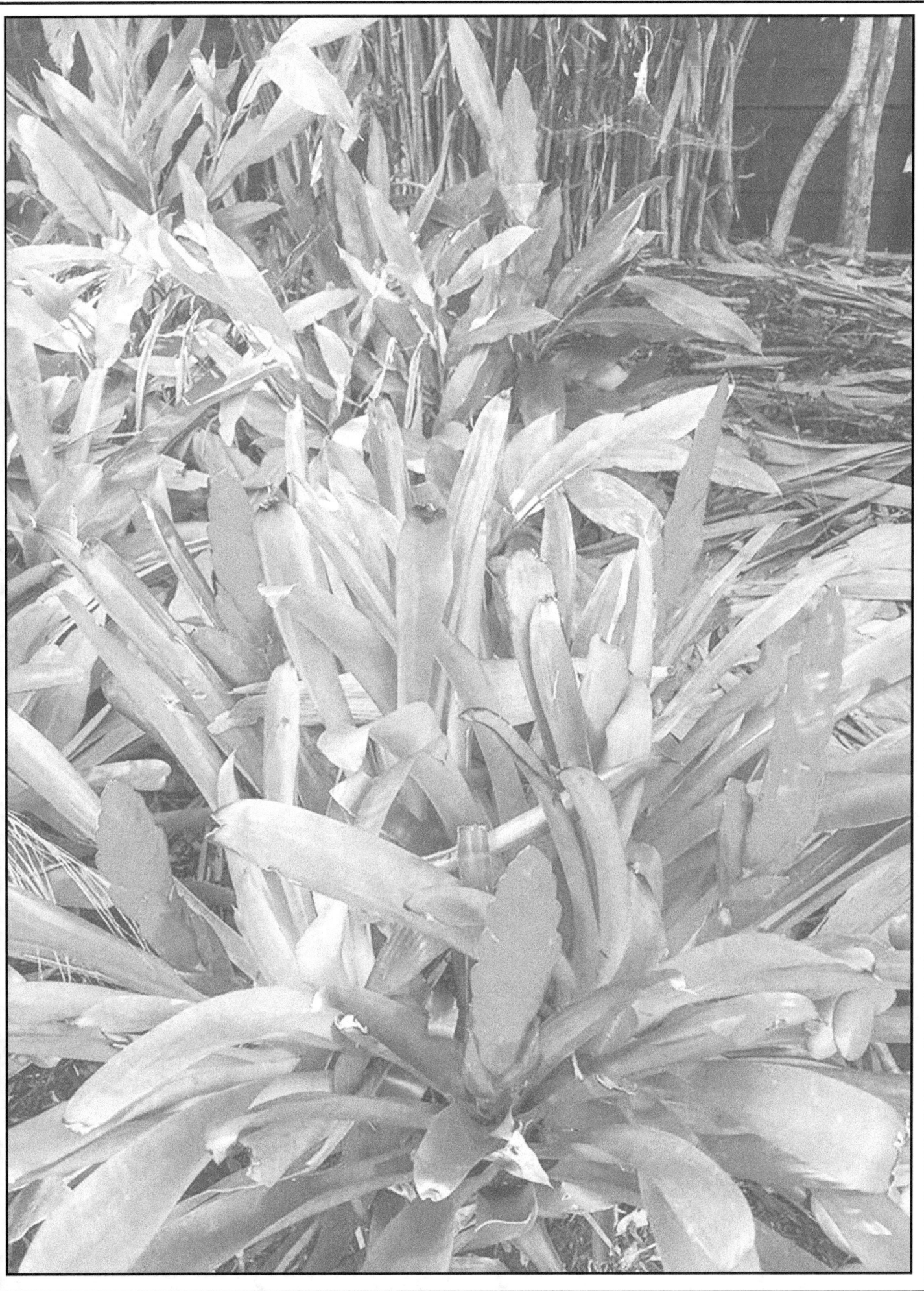

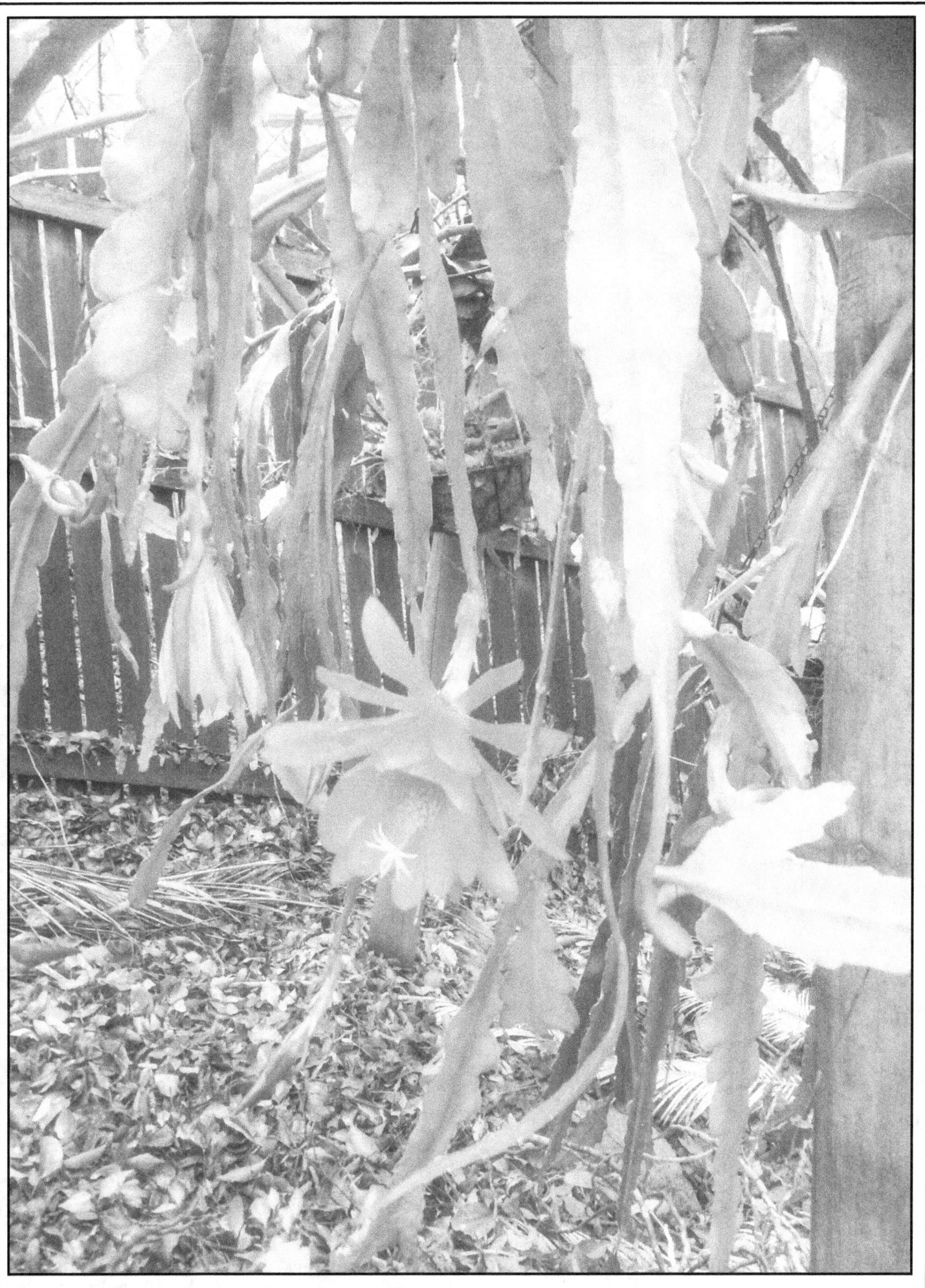

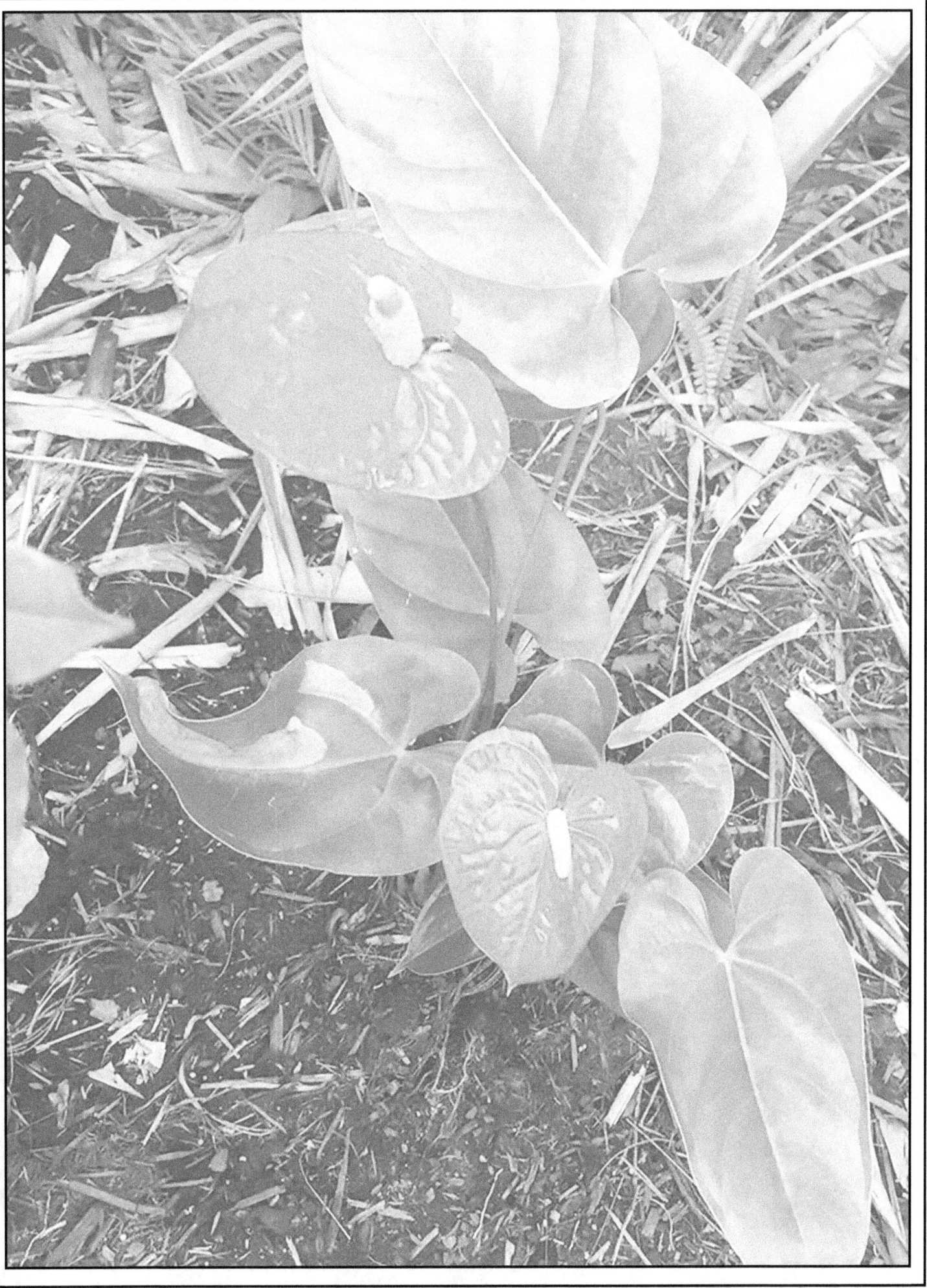

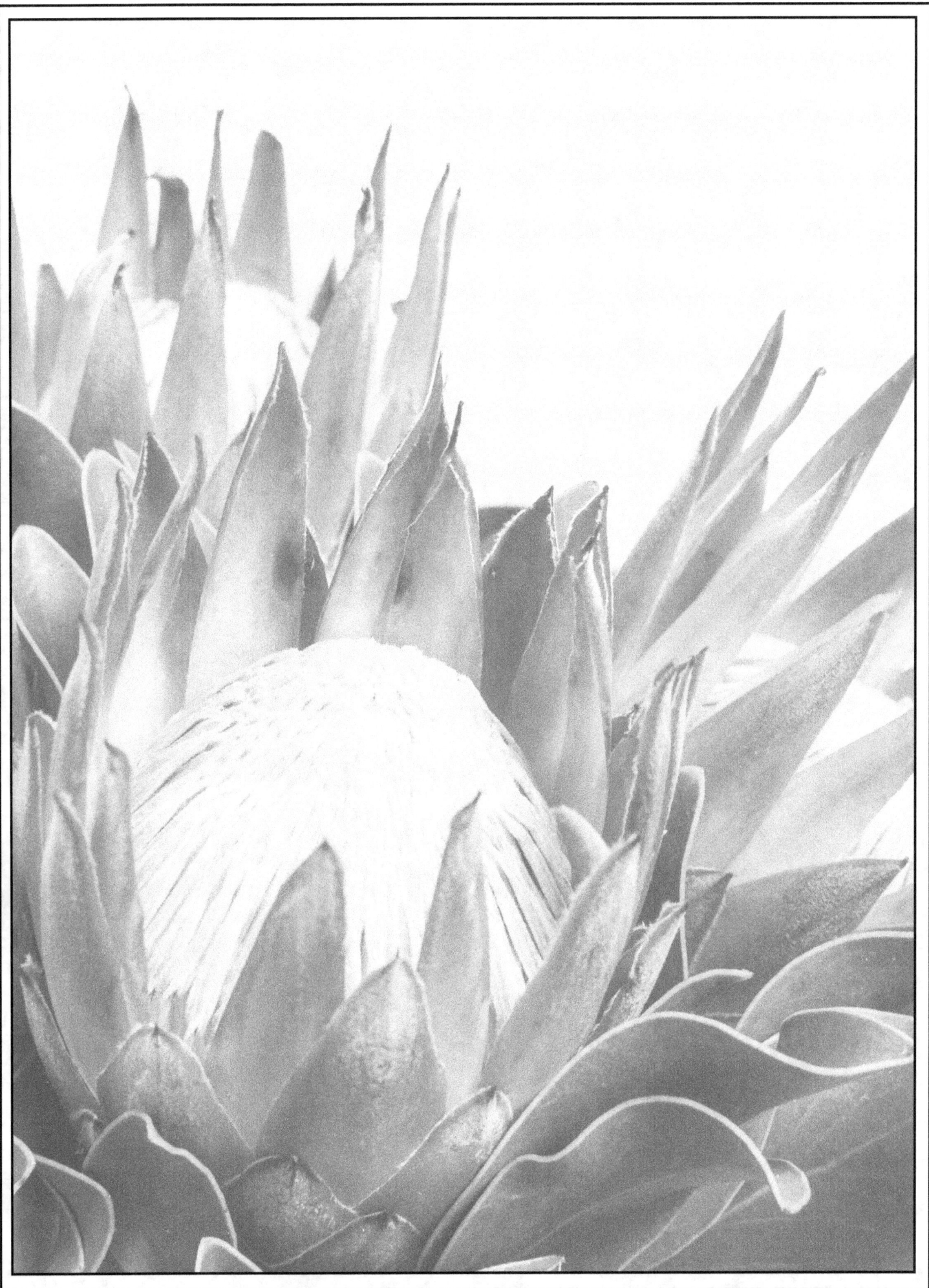

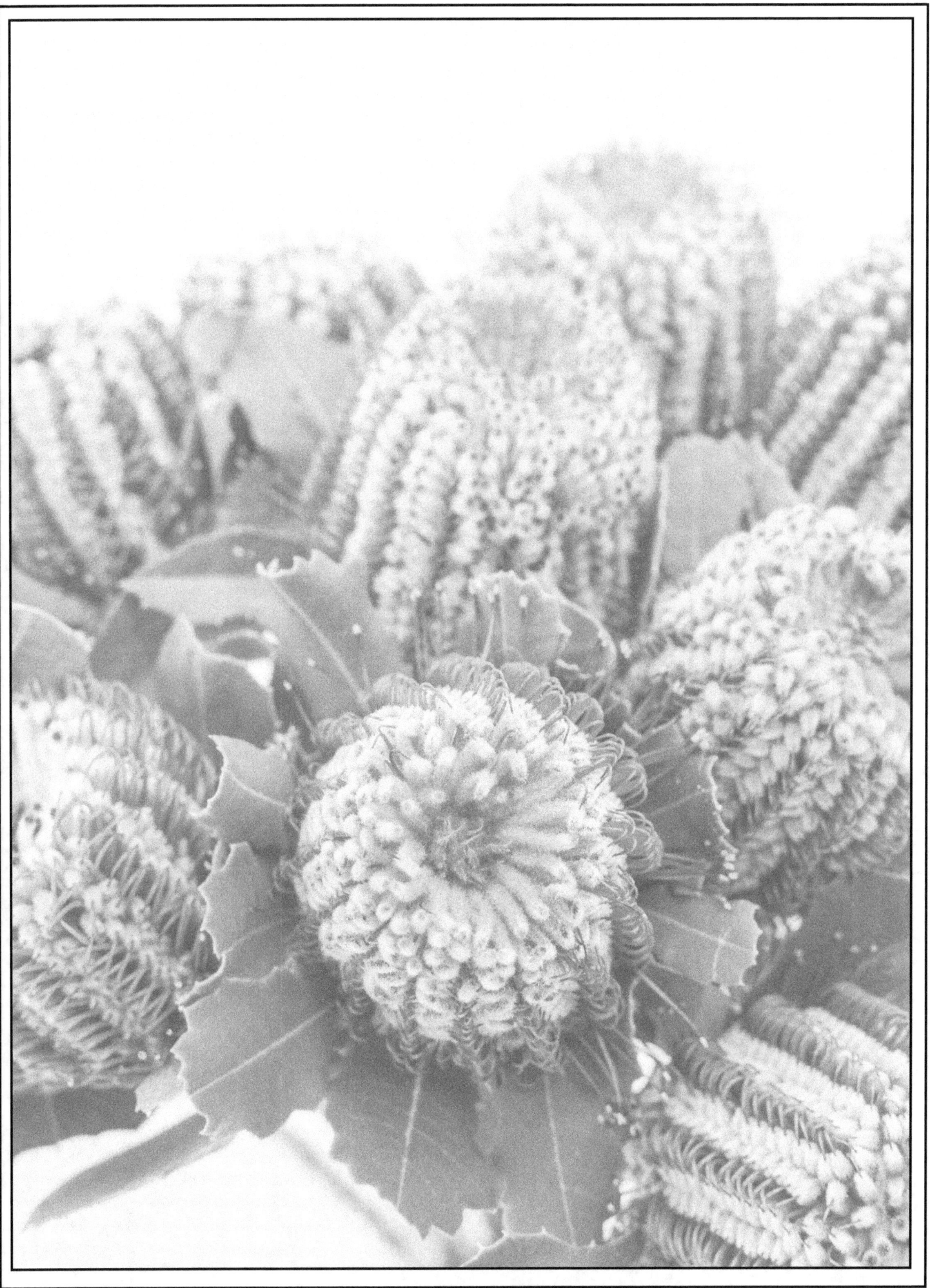

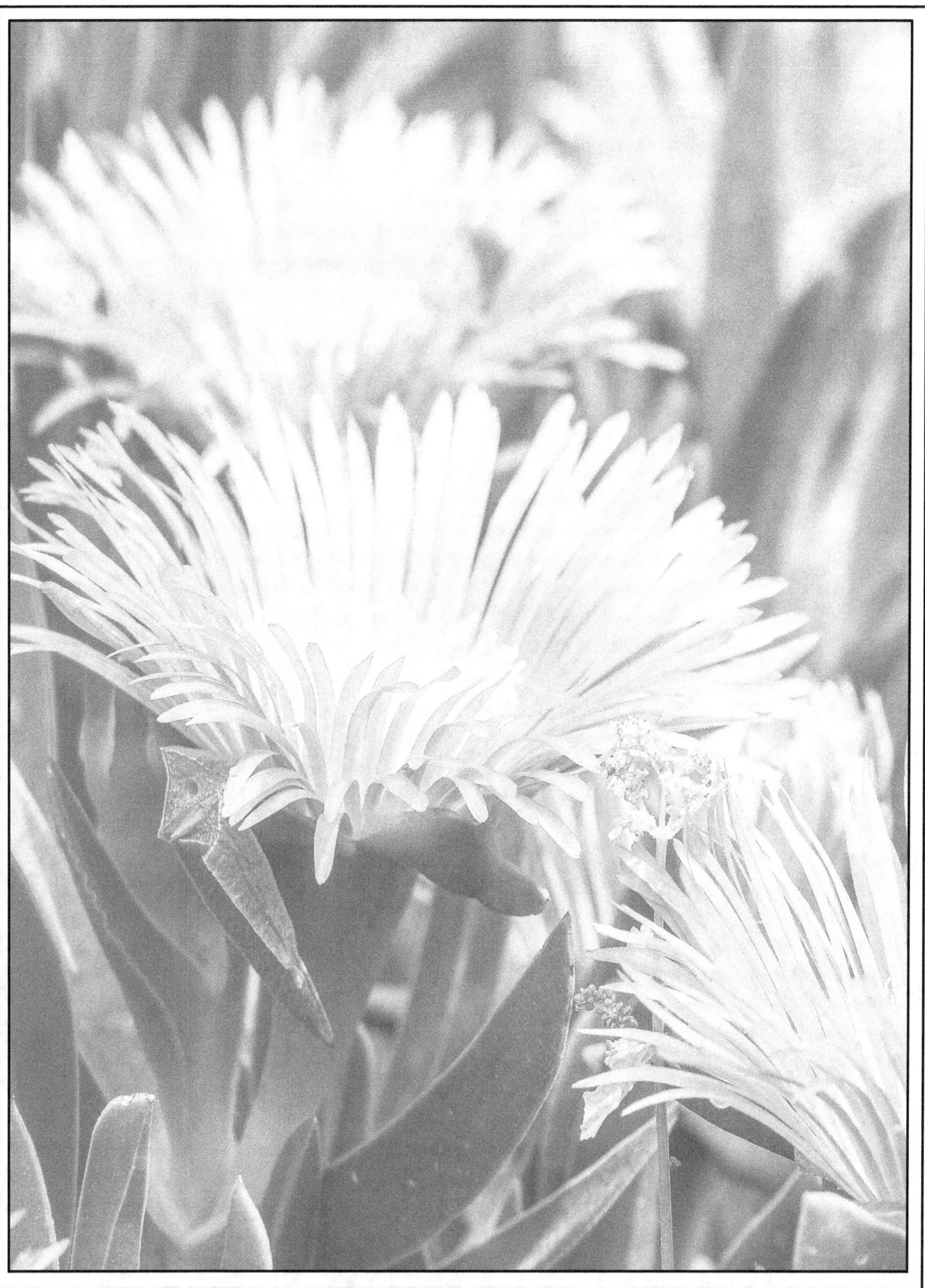

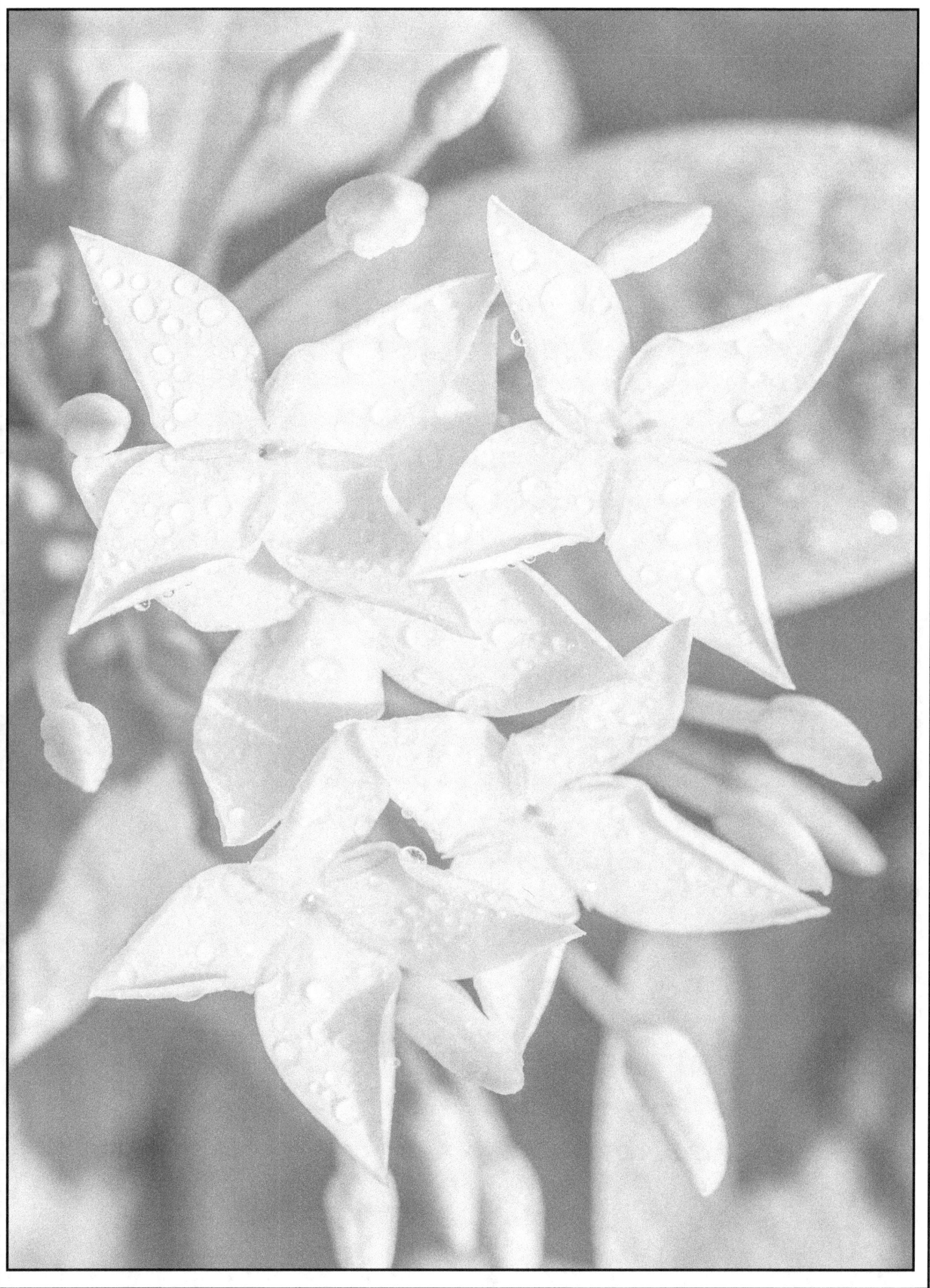

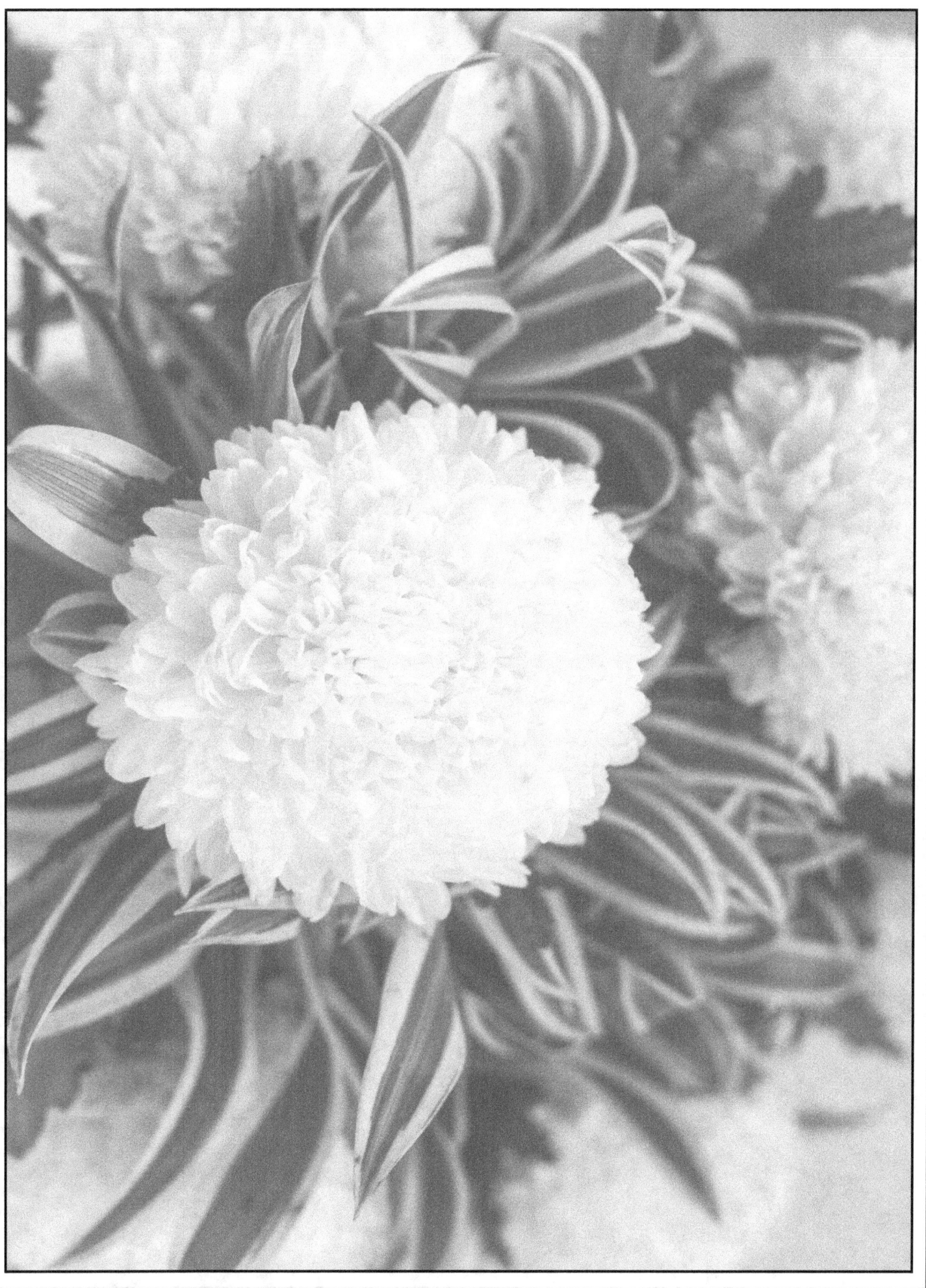

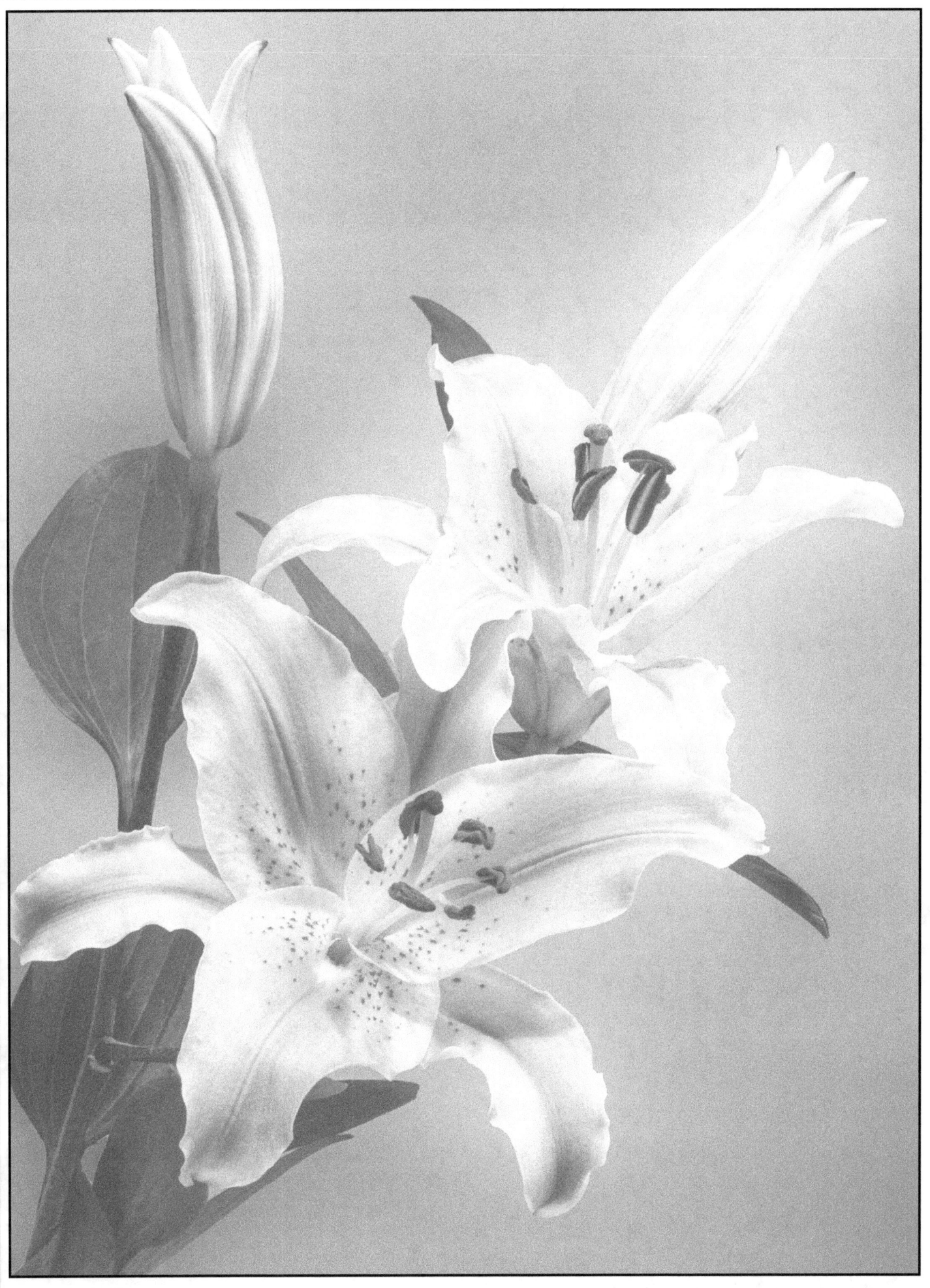

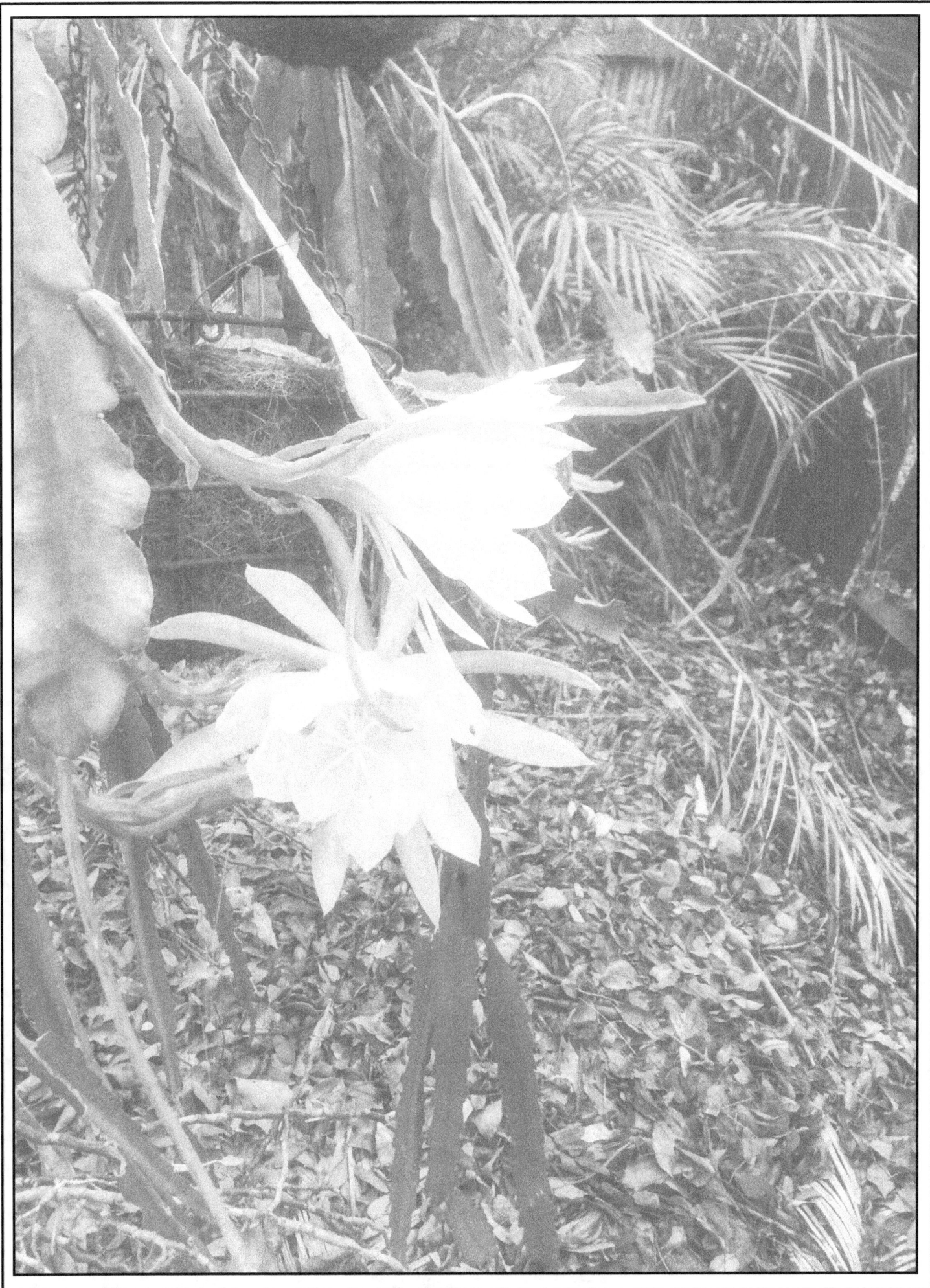

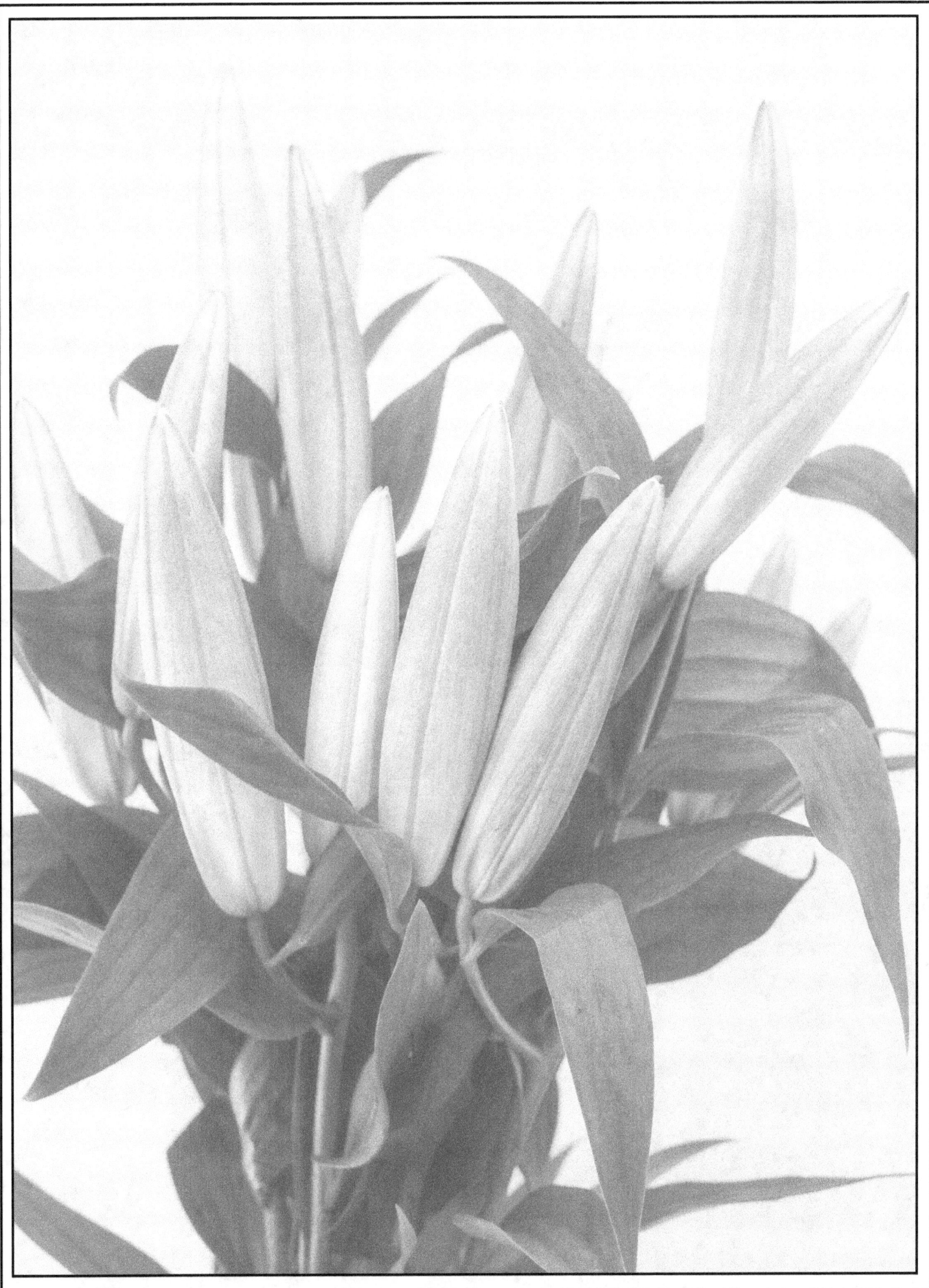

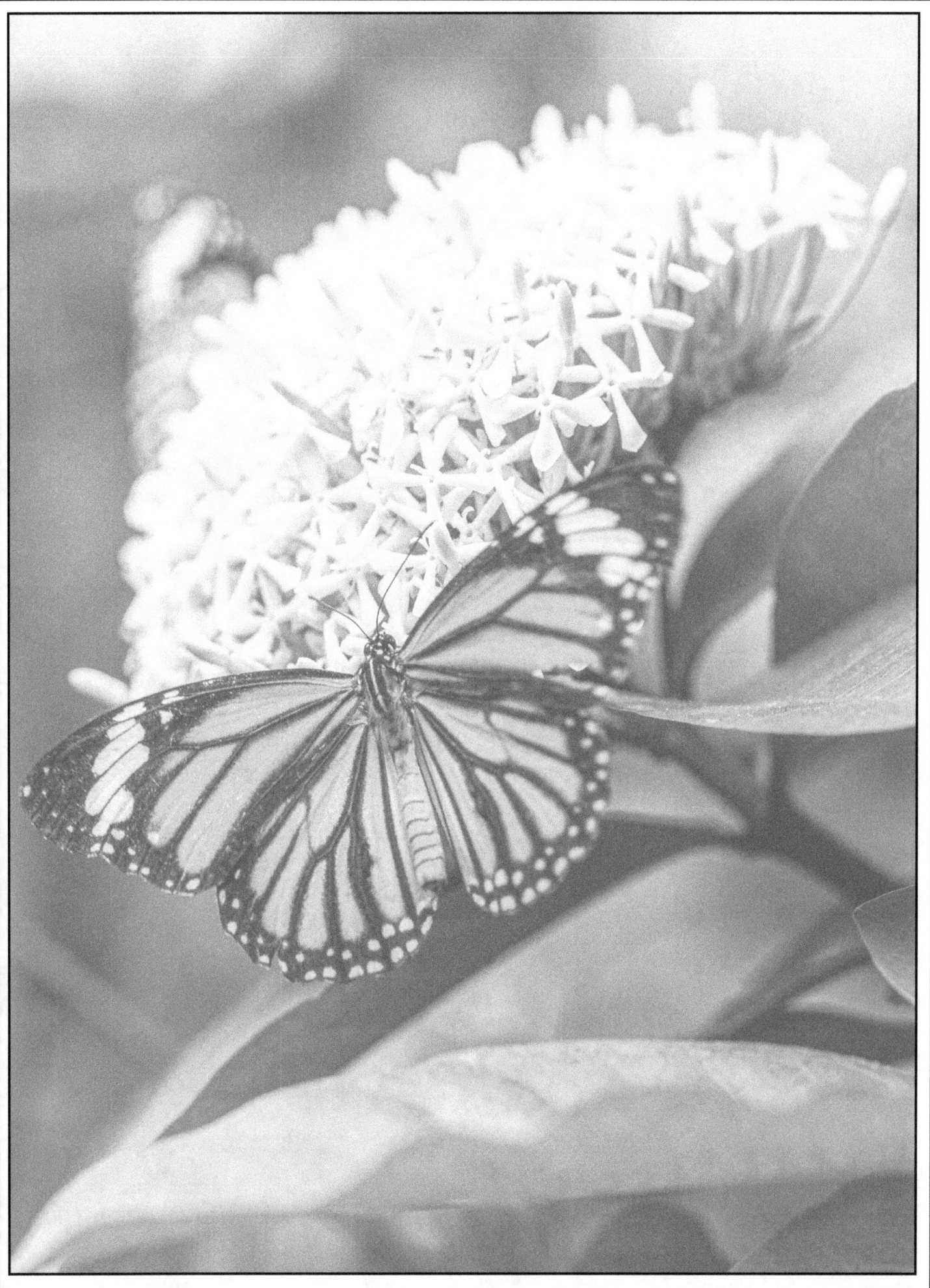

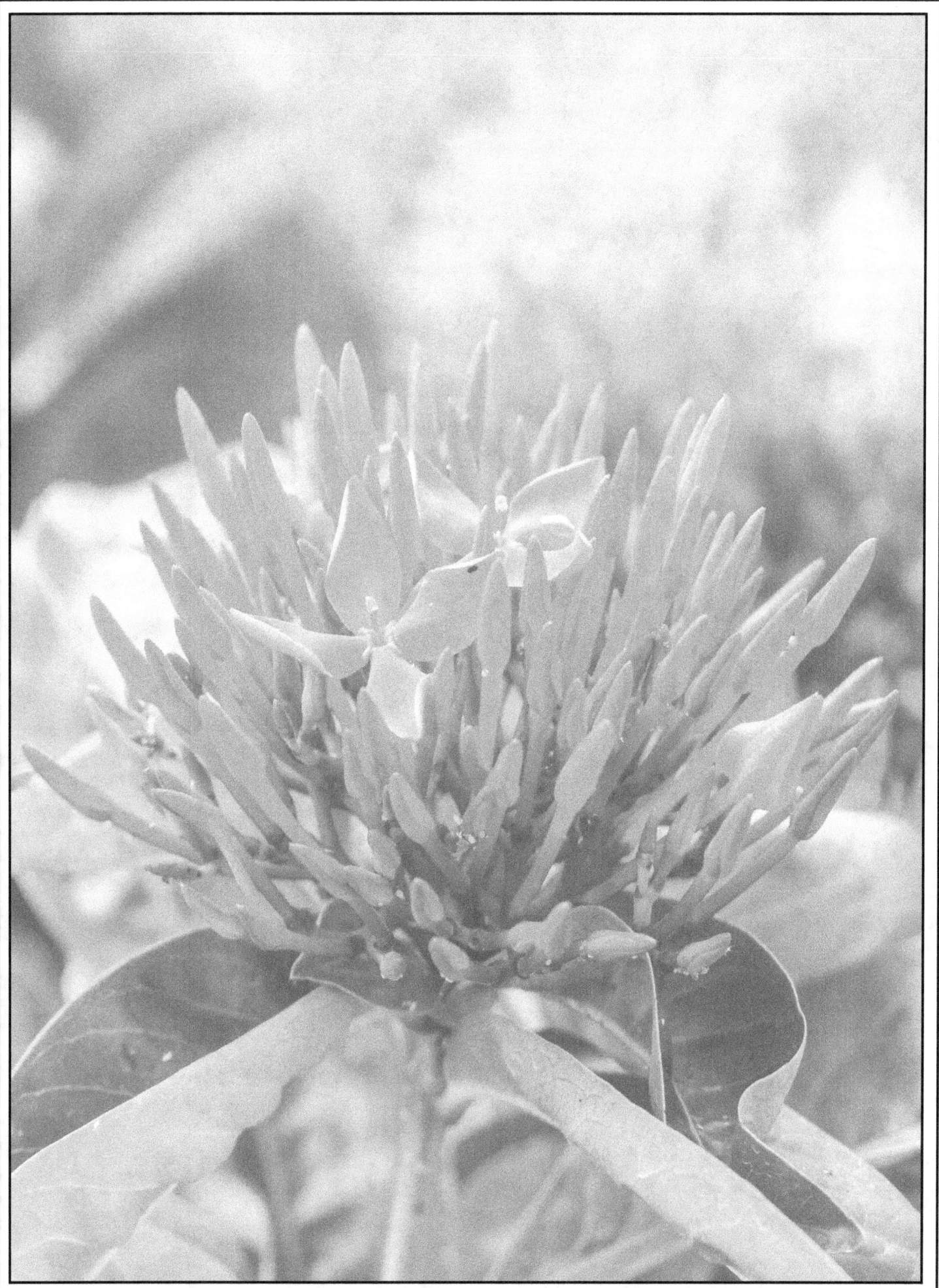

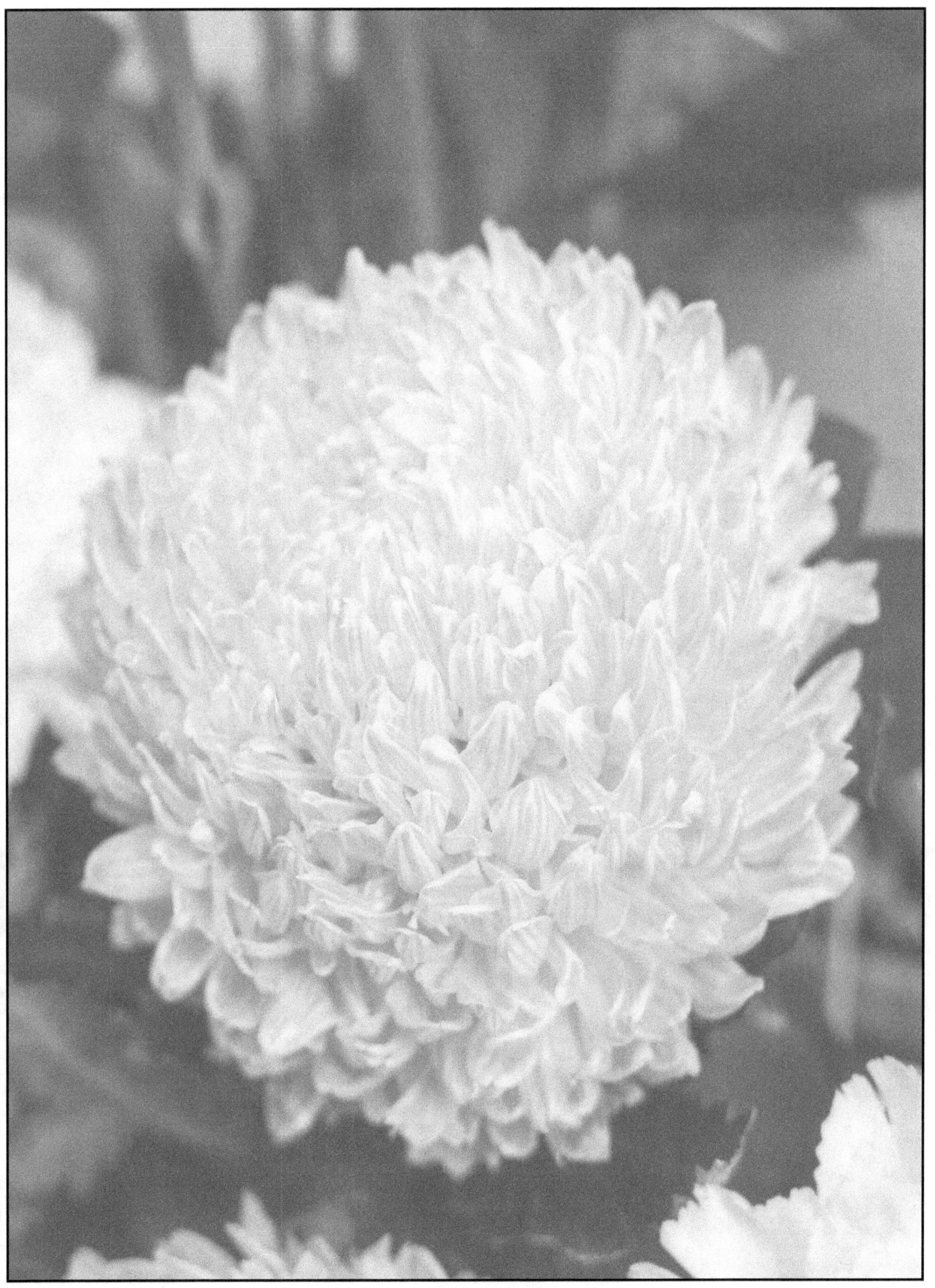

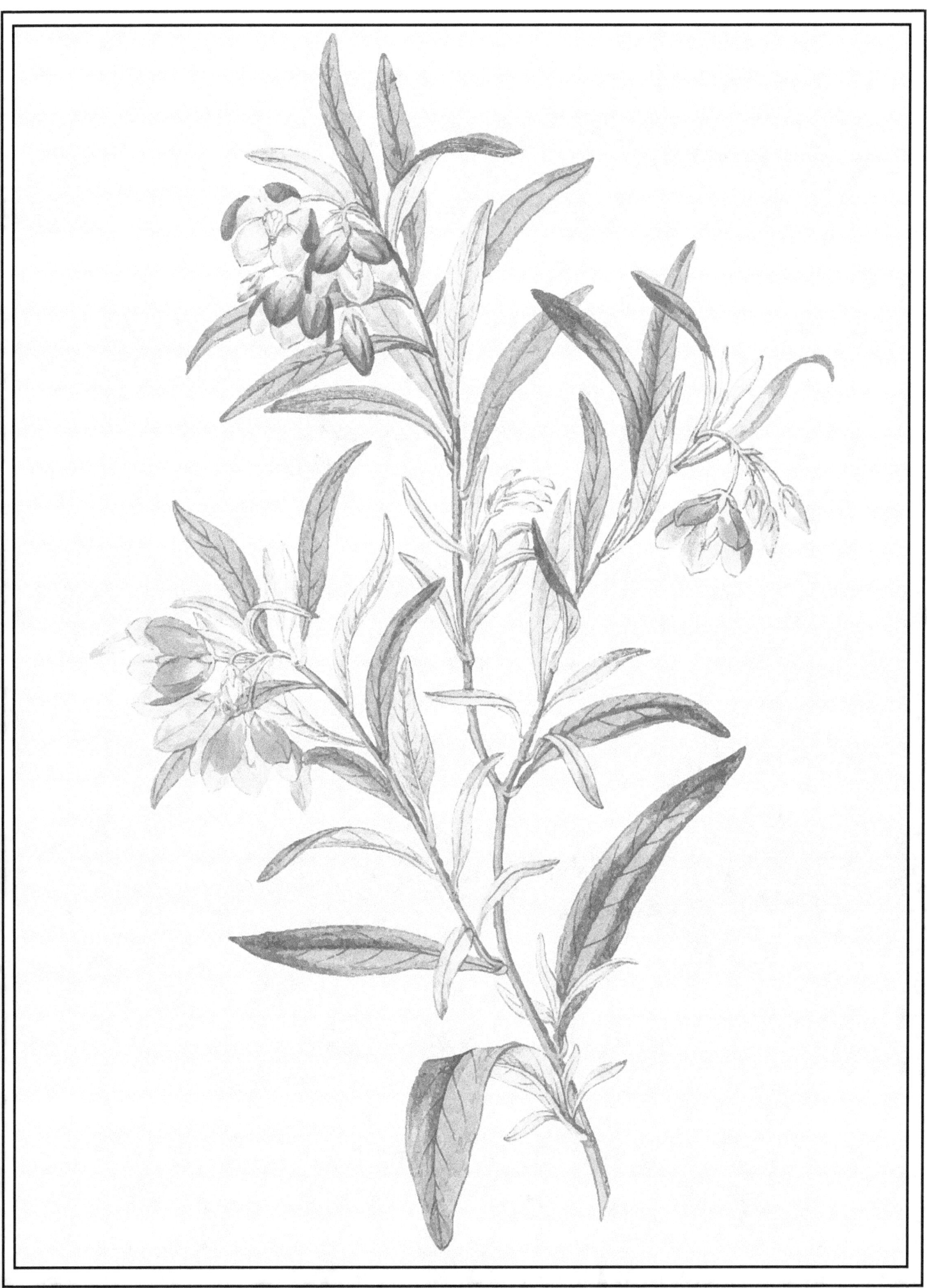

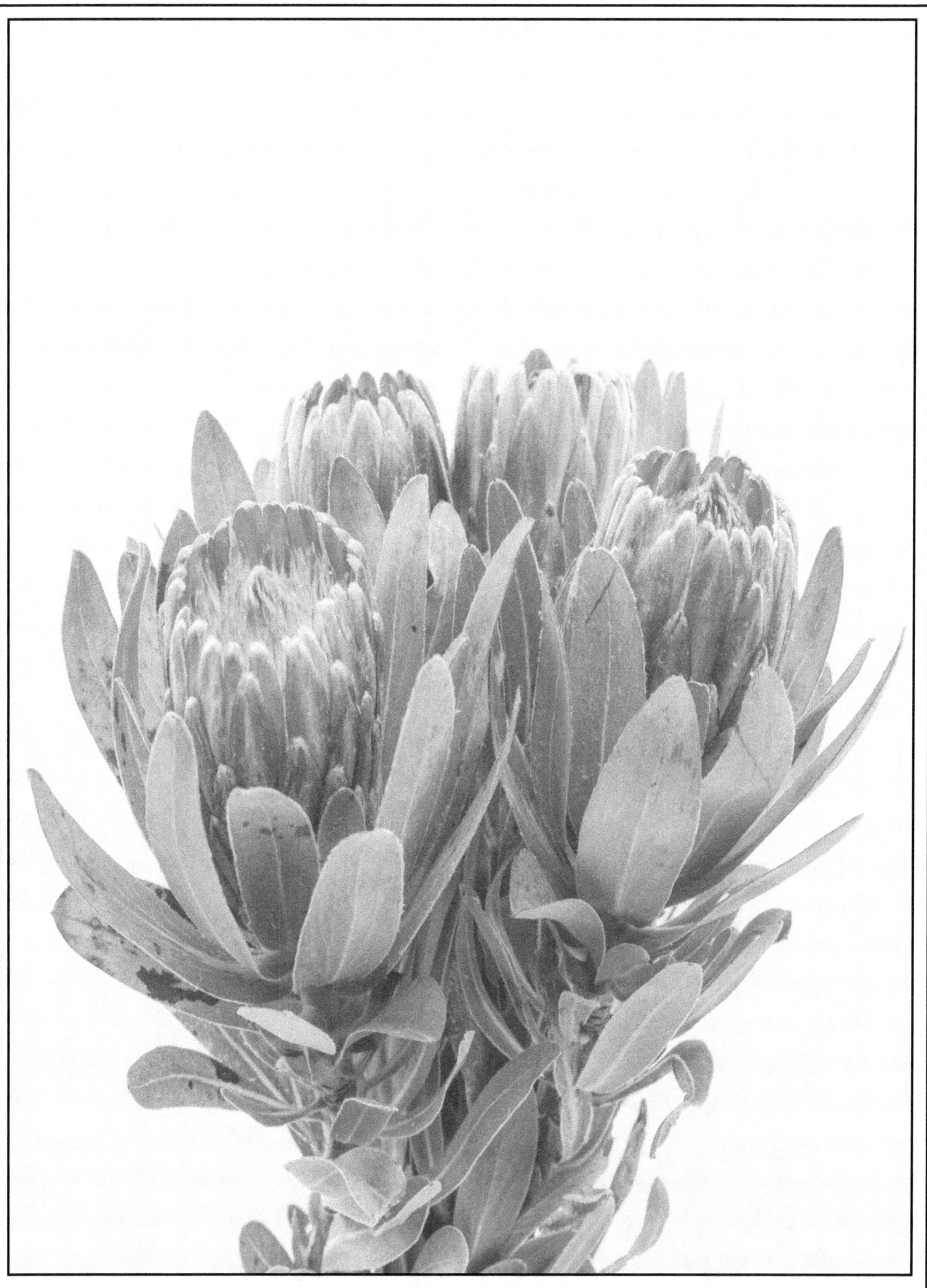

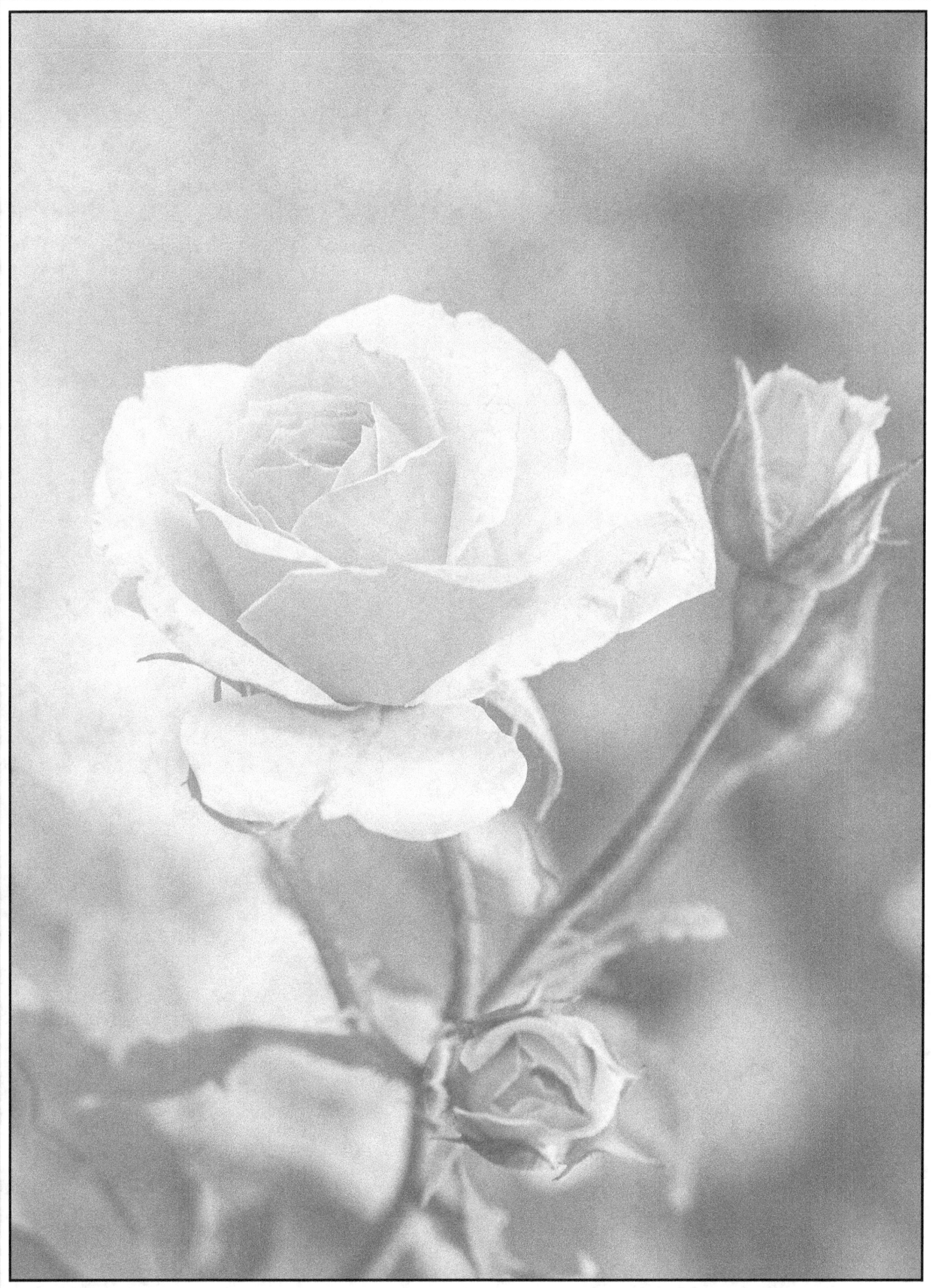

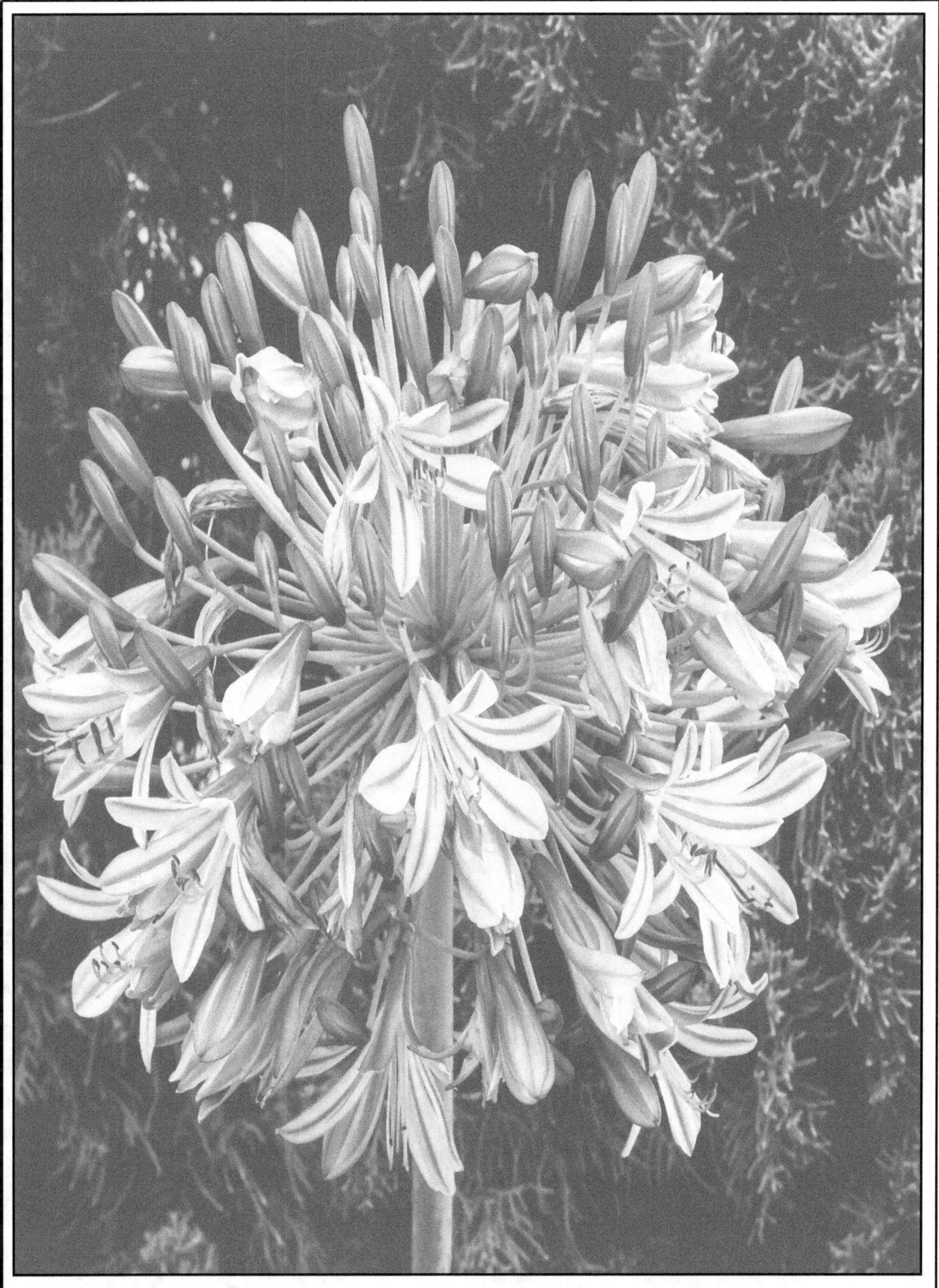

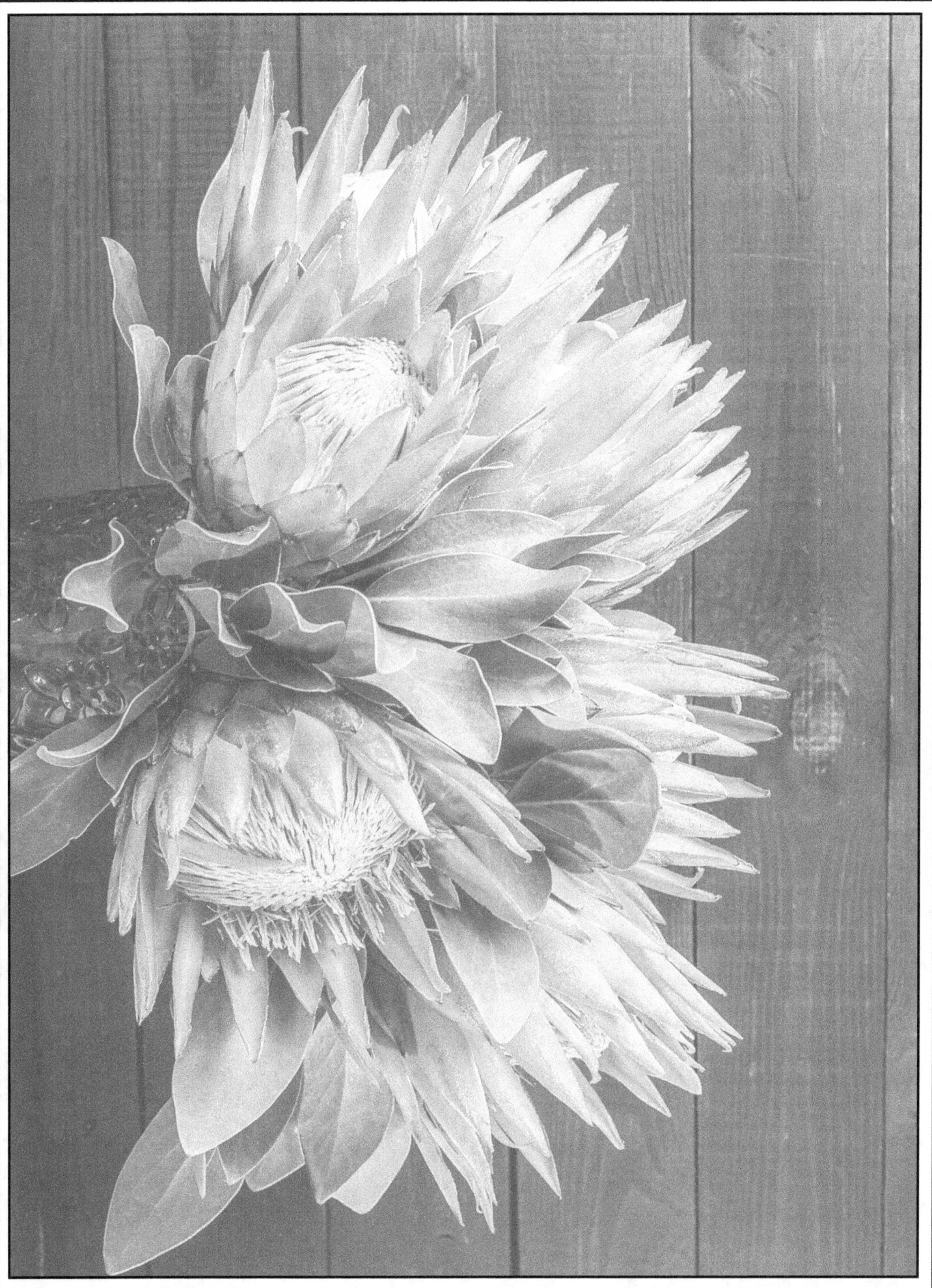

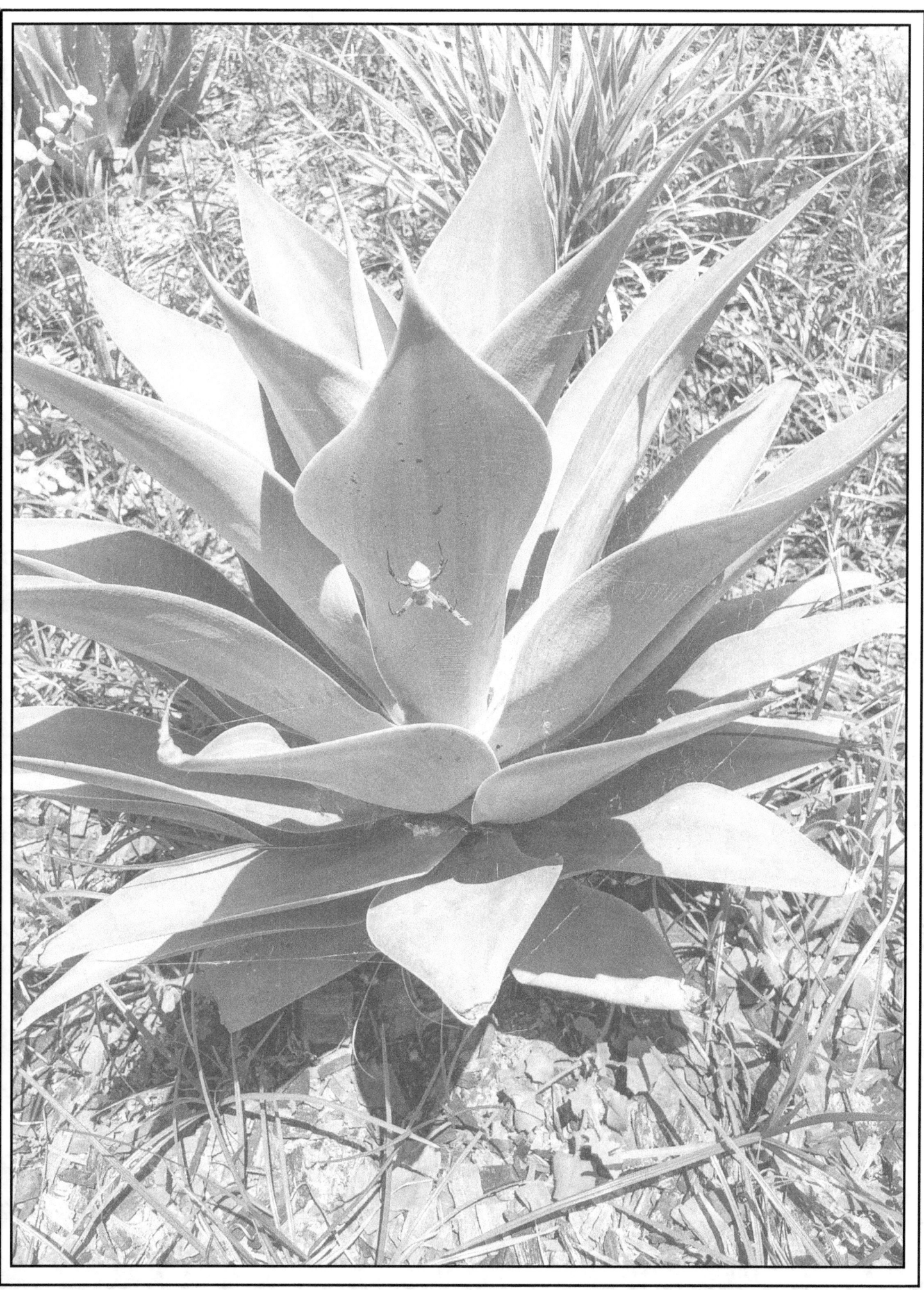

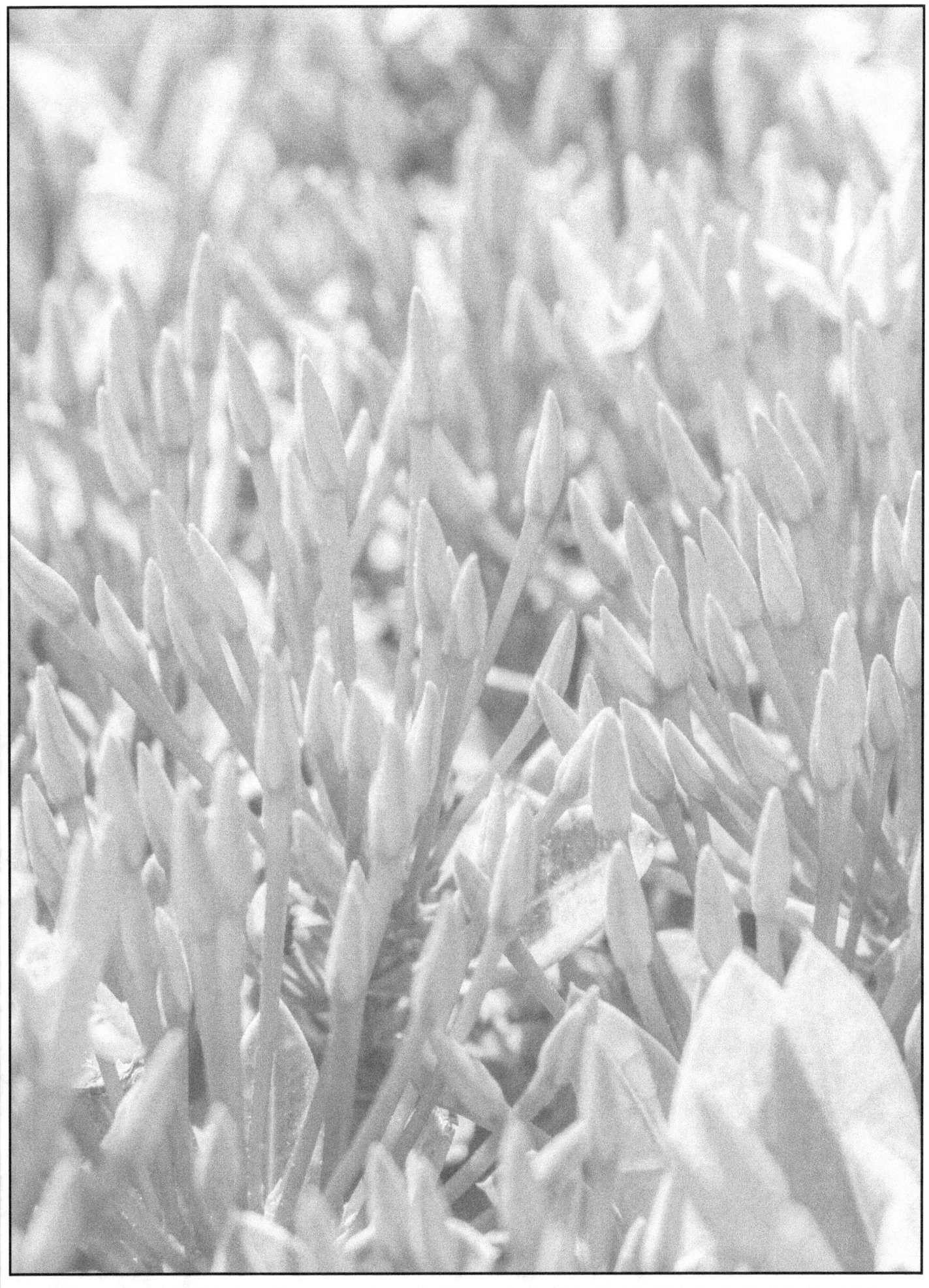

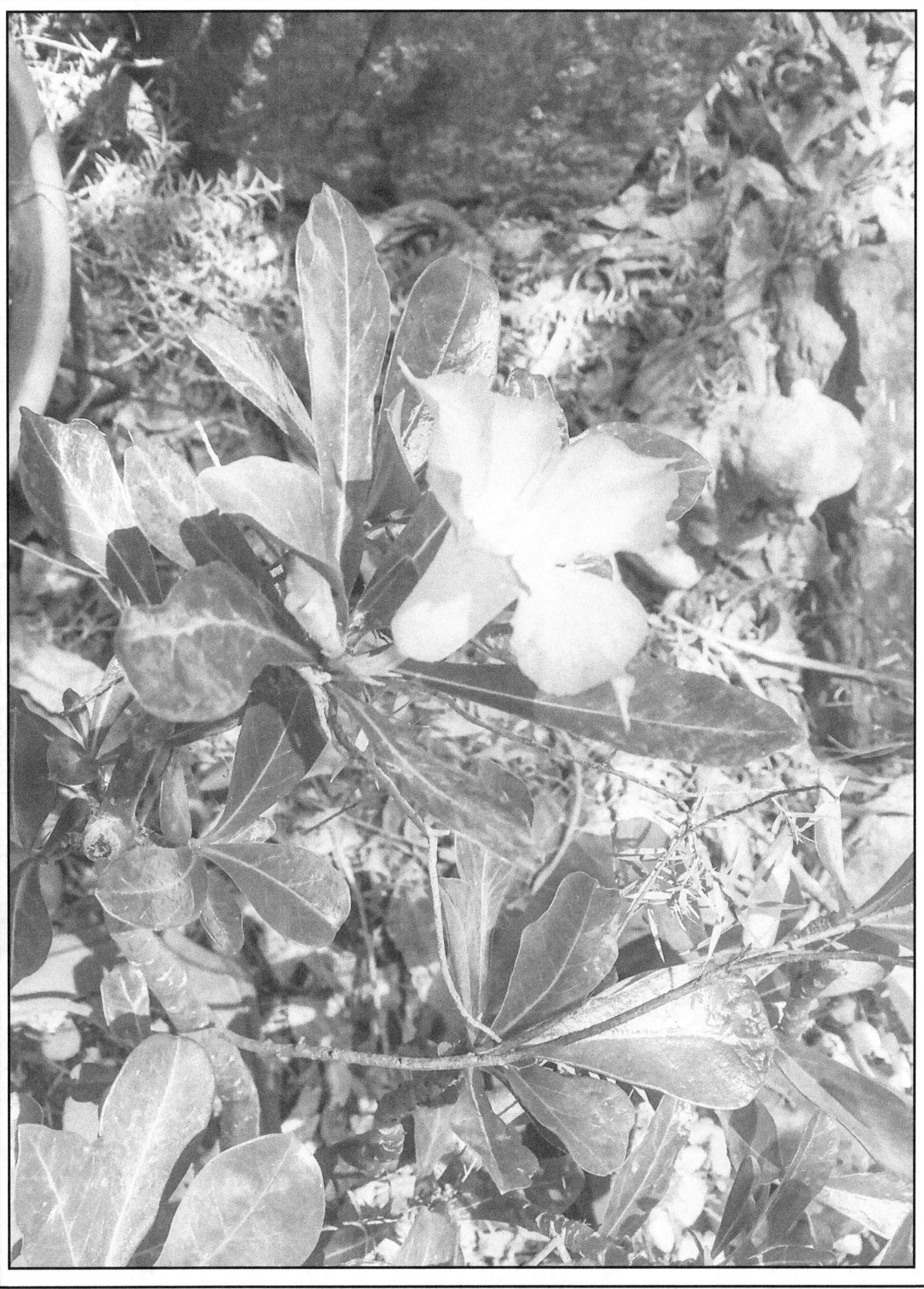

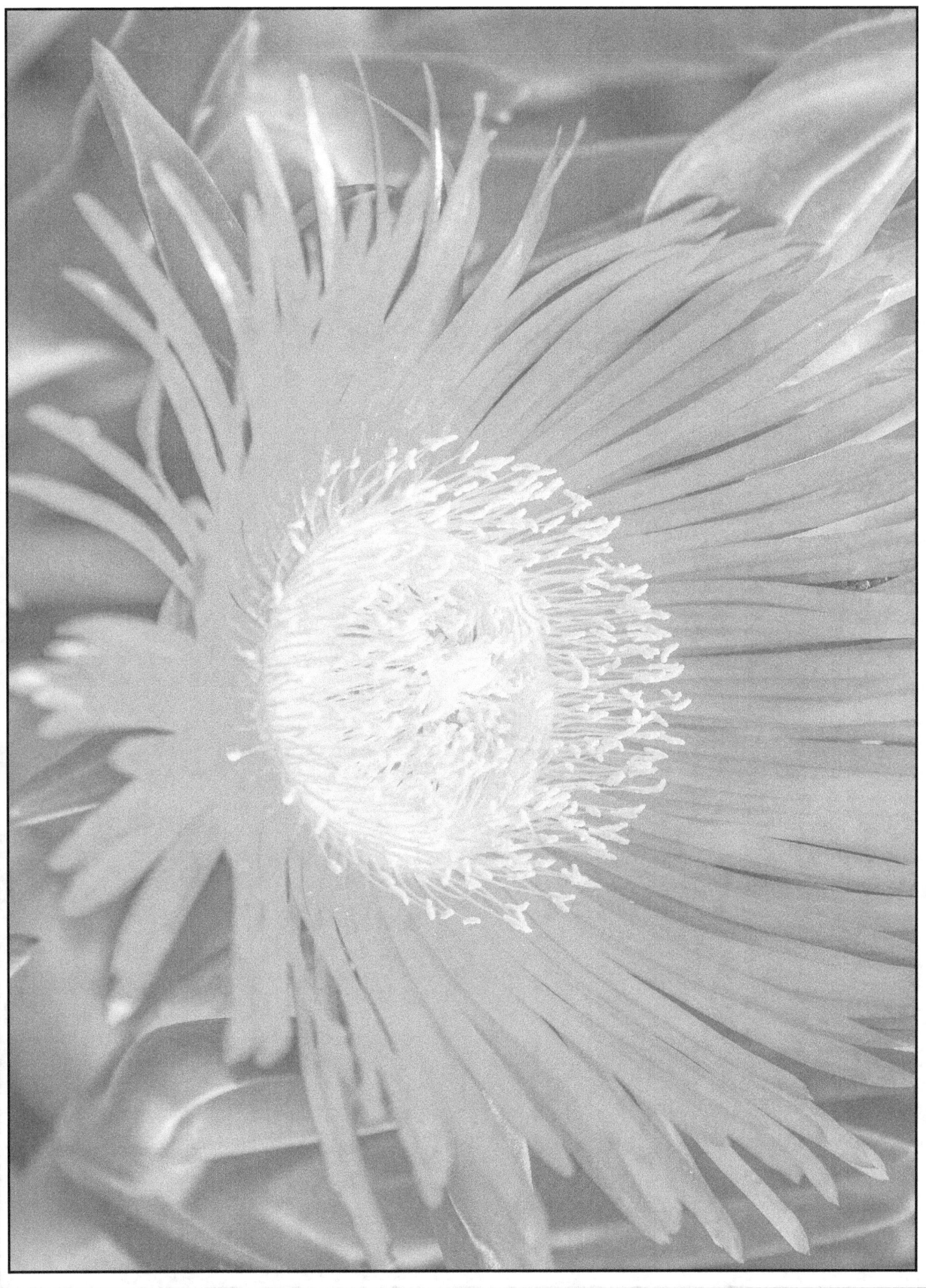